# GETTING AWAY WITH MURDER

## Political killings and 'disappearances' in the 1990s

AI Index: ACT 33/25/93

ISBN: 0 86210 225 1

First published: October 1993

Amnesty International
    Publications
1 Easton Street
London WC1X 8DJ
United Kingdom

Printed by:
    Flashprint Enterprises Ltd.

# CONTENTS

# ACRONYMS

| | |
|---|---|
| AFL | Armed Forces of Liberia |
| ANC | African National Congress |
| BLDP | Buddhist Liberal Democratic Party [Cambodia] |
| CAFGU | Citizen Armed Force Geographical Unit [Philippines] |
| CCB | Civil Cooperation Bureau [South Africa] |
| CHDF | Civilian Home Defense Force [Philippines] |
| CONADEP | National Commission on Disappeared People [Argentina] |
| CVOs | Civilian Self Defense Organizations [Philippines] |
| ECOWAS | Economic Community of West African States |
| ELN | National Liberation Army [Colombia] |
| ETA | Basque Homeland and Liberty |
| FARC | Revolutionary Armed Forces of Colombia |
| FRUD | Front for the Restoration of Unity and Democracy [Djibouti] |
| GAM | Mutual Support Group for the Appearance of our Relatives Alive [Guatemala] |
| HEP | People's Labour Party [Turkey] |
| IACHR | Inter-American Commission on Human Rights |
| ICRC | International Committee of the Red Cross |
| IKF | Iraqi Kurdistan Front |
| IRA | Irish Republican Army |
| JNA | Yugoslav National Army |
| LAPD | Los Angeles Police Department [USA] |
| LTTE | Liberation Tigers of Tamil Eelam |
| MAS | Death to Kidnappers [Colombia] |
| MRTA | Túpac Amaru Revolutionary Movement [Peru] |
| NPA | New People's Army [Philippines] |
| NPFL | National Patriotic Front of Liberia |
| PCP | Communist Party of Peru (Shining Path) |
| PDRY | People's Democratic Republic of Yemen |
| PKK | Kurdish Workers' Party |
| PLO | Palestine Liberation Organization |
| RENAMO | Mozambique National Resistance |
| RPF | Rwandese Patriotic Front |
| SLORC | State Law and Order Restoration Council [Myanmar] |
| SOC | State of Cambodia |
| SPLA | Sudan People's Liberation Army |
| STF | Special Task Force [Sri Lanka] |
| UDA | Ulster Defence Association |
| UK | United Kingdom |
| ULIMO | United Liberation Movement for Democracy in Liberia |
| UMOPAR | Mobile Rural Police [Bolivia] |
| UN | United Nations |
| UNITA | National Union for the Total Independence of Angola |
| USA | United States of America |
| UVF | Ulster Volunteer Force |
| YAR | Yemen Arab Republic |

# INTRODUCTION

*"The great mass murderers of our time have accounted for no more than a few hundred victims. In contrast, states that have chosen to murder their own citizens can usually count their victims by the carload lot. As for motive, the state has no peers, for it will kill its victim for a careless word, a fleeting thought, or even a poem."*

Dr Clyde Snow, a forensic anthropologist who analysed skeletal remains to expose atrocities committed by state officials in several countries.

Mass murderers are still on the loose. They are called governments and the scale of their crimes defies belief.

Every single day people are being murdered by government forces. They are being killed for their political views, for belonging to a particular community, or simply for being poor. Every day, too, people seized by government agents are facing another form of elimination when they vanish into secret custody as if they never existed. They "disappear".

Millions of men, women and children have suffered such fates since the 1960s — the victims not of wars between nations, but of deliberate government policies of repression. Their deaths or "disappearances" were ordered or condoned by state officials, the very people entrusted to protect their lives and liberty.

When Amnesty International last launched major campaigns against political killings and "disappearances" over 10 years ago, the world was haunted by some of the worst mass killings ever recorded.

Government troops and militia had butchered more than half a million civilians in Indonesia in the mid-1960s during an "anti-communist" pogrom. A similar campaign against the left in Chile resulted in the "disappearance" or murder of more than 2,000 people after General Pinochet seized power in 1973. In Pol Pot's so-called Democratic Kampuchea (Cambodia), at least 300,000 people were murdered in the "killing fields" between 1975 and 1979. Over 9,000 people "disappeared" under Argentina's military juntas in the late 1970s. In Ethiopia's worst year of "Red Terror" between 1977 and 1978, tens of thousands of civilians were murdered. In Idi Amin's Uganda, over a quarter of a million people were killed between 1972 and 1978.

Mass political killings and "disappearances" did not stop in the 1980s. In Iraq, for example, it is now known that hundreds of thousands of civilians, both Kurds and Arabs, were deliberately killed by security forces. In Syria, government forces killed several thousand people in just one incident in the town of Hama in 1982. In Uganda, hundreds of thousands more people were killed under the governments that followed Idi Amin's rule. In El Salvador, almost two per cent of the population is estimated to have been wiped out by "disappearances" and political killings during the civil war between 1980 and 1992. In Guatemala, entire villages were destroyed and tens of thousands of indigenous peasants were summarily executed as potential insurgents. In Chad, President Hissein Habré's regime murdered around 40,000 people.

Since then, dramatic political change has swept through whole continents. In many places, democratically elected governments replaced the military juntas and dictatorial regimes which had committed the worst violations. Governments in countries whose rulers did not even pay lip service to human rights a decade ago are now advocating respect for these fundamental rights. Some have brought their laws into line with international standards or have promised to do so. Many have established new institutions to promote and protect human rights.

In the excitement of all this change, a "new world order" was announced that promised an era in which governments would be accountable to their people and to national and international law, and would show greater respect for human rights at home and abroad.

This report shows that such promises were hollow. Tens of thousands of people are still being murdered every year by government agents or are "disappearing" without trace.

In countries such as China, Iraq and Myanmar, where gross human rights violations continue unabated, the governments do not even pretend to be accountable. Some of the worst violations,

*Two mass graves unearthed in 1981 at Cheng Ek, Kandal Province, Cambodia — just one of the many "killing fields" in which hundreds of thousands of people were slaughtered by Pol Pot's forces in the 1970s.*

*A Serb volunteer pumps bullets into a dying man after fighting had broken out between Serb and Muslim forces in the town of Brcko, northern Bosnia-Herzegovina, in May 1992. The victim had been lying injured without help for more than 24 hours. Thousands of civilians have been deliberately killed in the conflicts which have accompanied the break-up of former Yugoslavia. (c) Popperfoto/Reuters*

however, are taking place in countries ruled by governments which are ostensibly accountable to their own people and the international community, and which proclaim the sanctity of human rights.

In Sri Lanka, the formal structures of parliamentary democracy have done little to stop the security forces from carrying out tens of thousands of "disappearances" and political killings in the past decade. Colombia has remained a formal democracy throughout years of systematic and flagrant human rights violations by its security forces. In the Philippines, the formal restoration of democracy in 1986 has not prevented government and government-backed forces from butchering hundreds of unarmed civilians. In Peru, the election of successive civilian governments since 1980, all of which have promised to respect human rights, has coincided with an appalling level of political killings which has cost tens of thousands of lives in the past decade.

Moreover, gross human rights violations have continued or escalated in several countries which appeared to have finally reconciled warring factions or achieved political reform.

In Angola, for example, peace accords agreed by the government and the National Union for the Total Independence of Angola (UNITA) in 1991 have been repeatedly undermined by political violence and massive human rights abuses by both sides. In Cambodia, political killings rose sharply in the second half of 1992 and

*Supporters of the African National Congress run for cover as security forces open fire on demonstrators in Ciskei "homeland" in September 1992, killing at least 29 people and injuring hundreds. (c) AP*

in the run-up to UN-brokered elections in May 1993, and continued after they were held. In South Africa, horrific levels of bloodshed have accompanied the political reform process aiming to end the era of *apartheid*. Since 1990, when the process began, some 10,000 South Africans have been killed as a consequence of the actions of the security forces or, more frequently, as a consequence of the actions of armed groups acting with their acquiescence.

Elsewhere, the human rights situation has seriously deteriorated in the 1990s.

In former Yugoslavia, the human rights tragedy is on a scale that is hard to comprehend. Thousands of civilians have been deliberately and arbitrarily killed by members of Serb and Croat forces as well as by members of the largely Muslim Bosnian government forces in the fighting which has accompanied the break-up of Yugoslavia, particularly in Bosnia-Herzegovina where armed conflict has been raging since April 1992.

In Algeria, the government has recently adopted sweeping repressive measures to confront violent Islamic groups. In the first six months of 1993, over 300 government opponents and others were killed by the security forces, some of them victims of apparent extrajudicial executions, in the face of a rising tide of assassinations by Islamic militants. A sharp escalation in political killings by government forces has also been seen in Egypt and Turkey since 1992 in the context of rising armed opposition and assassinations by opposition forces.

In almost all these countries, legal and political institutions exist which should ensure that perpetrators of human rights violations are held accountable for their actions. Yet time and again, governments fail to show sufficient political will to bring to justice those who commit human rights crimes.

Moreover, in today's international climate of increased awareness of human rights issues, many governments rely on sophisticated cover-ups, blatant lies and covert methods of repression in order to perpetuate the terror while presenting a respectable face to the international community.

Some use methods of murder which attempt to conceal the crime. Killings are carried out by night, when the victims are alone. Bodies are mutilated and hidden to avoid identification and discovery. In places such as Afghanistan, Chad, Ethiopia, Eritrea, Iraq and Zimbabwe, recently uncovered mass graves have revealed thousands of victims of past political killings.

Governments distort the truth to blame others for political killings. Many try and blur the status of the killers, claiming they are civilian forces acting beyond their control. Mounting evidence shows that ostensibly civilian forces often work in close cooperation with the state or are, in fact, official forces operating in disguise. In the Philippines and Peru, official civil defence militia have participated in joint operations with conventional forces. In Sri Lanka and several Latin American countries, the authorities have attributed political killings to shadowy "death squads" which are actually made up of or supported by members of the armed forces. In South Africa there is a growing body of evidence linking "hit squads" responsible for political killings with covert police and military operations.

Armed conflict is frequently the pretext, as well as the context, for mass killings by official forces. Civilian deaths are justified by officials as the inevitable consequence of counter-insurgency operations. Massacres by security forces are blamed on rebels or insurgent groups. Prisoners are said to have been killed when trying to escape. It is often difficult to unravel the truth as access to areas of conflict is limited. In these circumstances governments feel less pressure to stop the violations.

In many countries governments do face a serious challenge from armed opposition groups which themselves use terror and deliberate killings in their campaigns. All too often, however, these governments have responded not with responsible measures to contain and control the violence, but by using it as an excuse for vicious repression. Ironically, one result of this may be to stoke up the fires of bitterness and make lasting peace even harder to achieve.

Many of the worst cases of mass political killings and "disappearances", however, have occurred in countries where the supposed conflict was all but invisible to the outside observer. In Guatemala, for example, the army has murdered tens of thousands of people since the 1960s in a campaign which officials have justified as a response to a guerrilla movement which at times was barely operational. In Iraq, the security forces have continued to commit gross human rights violations in areas where mass terror has virtually wiped out active opposition.

Governments often present political killings as the legitimate result of law enforcement when, in reality, the action taken goes far beyond the limits of the law. Executions after secret, summary trials

— or no trials at all — flout international standards protecting human rights, yet are presented as lawful executions. In Iran, at least 2,500 prisoners were summarily and arbitrarily executed in 1988, while government secrecy made it impossible to determine whether trials had ever taken place.

In dozens of countries, the police and security forces routinely use grossly excessive force in response to demonstrations, in many cases deliberately killing unarmed civilians in order to make a political point. Official accounts of such incidents often blame the protesters for starting the violence.

The official lies and covert methods cloud the extent to which the terror is continuing in the "new world order". In addition to the countries where mass political killings have continued for decades, there are many others where hundreds or thousands of people have been victims of "disappearance" or extrajudicial execution in recent years. They include Burundi, China, Indonesia, Somalia and Sudan. Since the beginning of 1992, Amnesty International has recorded "disappearances" and political killings in more than 60 countries.

The trend has not been universally for the worse, however. Some countries have dramatically improved their human rights records, such as Chile and Zimbabwe, although even in these countries violations continue and governments have either failed to investigate past "disappearances" and political killings or have failed to bring those responsible to justice. In other countries, new governments have made genuine efforts to end long-established patterns of violations.

Moreover, human rights have never had a higher profile internationally, a fact reflected in the proliferation of international and regional human rights treaties and other international standards which most governments have formally agreed and therefore undertaken to respect.

These developments should be a cause of great optimism and celebration. Yet the harsh truth is that they are entirely overshadowed by the governments that persist with ruthless repression and by the international community which allows so many states to get away with murder.

For the victims and their relatives, and for all those who live in constant fear for their lives, it is vital that the world wakes up to the continuing mass slaughter. One of the main tasks for human rights organizations must therefore be to expose the atrocities and unravel the official lies which hide human rights crimes behind a fog of disinformation and dishonest pledges.

This report aims to show some of the lives behind the lies. It hopes to convey the suffering experienced by ordinary people and whole communities when governments use terror to achieve their goals. It does this for one purpose only — to stimulate action. Action to stop "disappearances" and political killings in every country of the world.

The proliferation of nationalist, secessionist, ethnic and religious conflicts threatens all regions with violence and bloodshed. The international community has shown itself either unwilling or unable to bring about an end to injustice and brutality. Unless action is taken soon to stop political killings and "disappearances" wherever they occur, the rising tide of carnage could overwhelm the institutions set up to promote international human rights standards after the horrors of the Second World War. The losers, everywhere, would be ordinary men, women and children.

Human rights violations are not an inevitable part of modern society. They are the consequence of decisions taken by state officials. These officials must be forced to change their ways. Our job is to pile on the pressure until they have no choice but to take different decisions which can stop the violence.

This report is part of a campaign which hopes to mobilize the millions of ordinary people who want to see an end to political killings and "disappearances". The campaign is based on the firm belief that our actions can force governments to take steps to stop the terror at home and abroad. By acting together, we believe we can create a genuine "new world order" in which basic human rights are a reality for everyone, not just a privilege for the few.

# 1

# The terror

## What are 'disappearances' and political killings?

Early one morning in July 1992, Peruvian soldiers entered La Cantuta university campus on the outskirts of Lima and forced students to lie on the floor. They picked out at least nine young men and women and dragged them away. At the same time, hooded men snatched Hugo Muñoz Sánchez, a lecturer, from his home on the campus and took him away gagged and still in his night clothes. None was ever seen alive again. They "disappeared".

People are considered to have "disappeared", rather than to have simply gone missing, when there are reasonable grounds to believe that they have been taken into custody by state officials or with their connivance or acquiescence, and when the authorities then deny any knowledge about the victims' fate or whereabouts.

The students and lecturer who were abducted in Peru clearly fit this definition. Although they had clearly been taken away by soldiers, a judge rejected a petition for *habeas corpus* which had been filed on their behalf. He said it was inadmissible because the military denied that the missing people were being held at the two military bases from which the arresting soldiers would have come, and because their names were not entered in the registers of detainees at either base. In mid-1993, after a high ranking army officer had accused a special military intelligence unit of carrying out the abductions and subsequently murdering the victims (see Chapter 3), an Amnesty International research team of forensic pathologists witnessed and filmed the exhumation of the bodies of the students and lecturer from four mass graves.

Such cases highlight the powerlessness of

victims and the frustration faced by their families when governments condone "disappearances".

"Disappearances" are never random incidents. They need a high degree of organization involving many officials. The victim must be selected and located. Forces are needed to take the victim into custody. A system must be in place to ensure concealment, of both the victim and the records. Another system, involving many layers of officialdom, must exist to obstruct the efforts of families, friends, lawyers and human rights activists to find the "disappeared".

The need for concealment affects all procedures involved in "disappearances". Victims are often selected and tracked down by an official intelligence agency, whose activities are secret. The fact that the Lima students were singled out from among many forced to lie down implies that a list of wanted people was drawn up before the raid.

The abductions or arrests are sometimes carried out openly by officials who normally make arrests, such as police officers, but only if these forces enjoy such blatant power that they know they can act with impunity. More often, the victims are taken away by night, without witnesses, or by officials in disguise.

Efforts to locate victims are obstructed by anything from straight denial and refusal of access to detention centres to threats and intimidation. All of those involved in a "disappearance" are implicated in the crime and therefore do anything in their power to cover up the truth.

The fate of the "disappeared" varies from country to country and from period to period. Sometimes the victims are held in secret for many years — and then released without explanation. Tragically, however, "disappearances" are more usually a prelude to extrajudicial executions. Victims "disappear" and are then tortured to death or killed under the cover of their "disappearance". Officials still deny any knowledge of the missing person and the bodies are frequently disposed of secretly or mutilated beyond recognition.

The term extrajudicial executions, as used by Amnesty International, refers to unlawful and deliberate killings carried out by order of a government or with its complicity or acquiescence. In this report, the term "political killings" is also used as it is more easily understood and includes, in addition to murder by governments, deliberate and arbitrary killings by armed political groups often involved in opposition to governments.

Extrajudicial executions can be clearly distinguished from killings by the state which are within the law, or killings by other parties to an armed conflict which are consistent with international standards. For example, if someone dies as the result of soldiers acting in self defence, or of police during a riot using the minimum force strictly necessary to protect life, then the killing is tragic but not unlawful. Similarly, when a state carries out a death sentence imposed by a court after a fair trial, the killing is not unlawful — although in Amnesty International's view it is a violation of basic human rights and ought to be outlawed.

For a killing to be deemed an extrajudicial execution, it must also have been deliberate — in other words, not accidental — and committed with government involvement or acquiescence. If a soldier kills someone for personal reasons and the state sub-sequently punishes the soldier as it would any other murderer, the killing by the soldier was not an extrajudicial execution. By taking such action, the authorities show they neither condone nor tolerate the killing. If, however, an unlawful killing was a result of official orders or government policy, or committed by government-backed forces, or if the authorities refuse to investigate the crime or punish the perpetrator, so indicating their acquiescence, then it was an extrajudicial execution.

As with "disappearances", governments which order or con-done political killings not only conspire to break their own laws, they also conspire to pervert the course of justice so that the lawbreaking will go unpunished. Human rights organizations and independent investigators therefore face a barrage of obstacles to uncovering the truth about political killings and "disappearances". Lifting the fog of official misinformation is a crucial part of the campaign to make both governments and the international commu-nity face up to their responsibilities and take action to stop the terror.

## 'Disappearances'

Hundreds of thousands of friends and relatives of people who have "disappeared" hang on to what seems a remote, if not ridiculous, sense of hope. The story of three French-Moroccan brothers shows that such hope is not always misplaced.

Midhat, Bayazid and Ali Bourequat "disappeared" after arrest in Morocco in 1973. In December 1991 they suddenly reappeared,

*Midhat, Bayazid and Ali Bourequat at a press conference in January 1992 shortly after their release from an 18-year nightmare of secret detention in appalling conditions. They were among hundreds of Moroccans and Western Saharans who "disappeared" between 1963 and 1991. Their survival and eventual freedom offers hope to the thousands of relatives of the "disappeared" around the world who are still waiting for news.*

released from an underground hell called Tazmamert in the remote Atlas mountains in which they had spent the previous ten and a half years in total darkness. They had barely survived their long nightmare, yet there they were — against all the odds — alive.

Caroline Moorehead, a British journalist, described their first weeks of freedom:

> *"They are learning, painfully, how to walk again. Midhat, the eldest, who will be 60 next year, has lost more than ten inches in height and shuffles awkwardly, his head sunk deep into his shoulders, his neck almost vanished. The expression on his face is one of constant pain. Bayazid, the second brother, now 58, can pull himself to his feet only with his arms, his spine being so curved that he seems to be carrying an immense burden on his back. Of the three, only Ali, the youngest at 54, stands upright, but he too is frail and shrunken.... Few people have ever been subjected to such conditions; even fewer have ever survived."*

The Bourequat brothers were among hundreds of Moroccans and Western Saharans who "disappeared" between 1963 and 1991 after being detained by Moroccan government forces. Worldwide campaigns and international pressure eventually secured the release of over 300 of them in 1991. Hundreds of others, however, have never been heard of again. Some may have died, but most are believed still to be alive in secret detention.

The term "disappearance" ("*desaparecido*") first entered the human rights vocabulary in Guatemala in 1966, when the government began disposing of political opponents in secret. The practice was then adopted in several Latin American countries and, like some ghastly plague, had soon infected every continent in the world.

In Guatemala "disappearances" continued on a mass scale for more than 20 years. In the first decade of official terror, beginning in 1966, an estimated 20,000 people were victims of political killings and "disappearances" by clandestine army-backed "death squads", regular police and military forces, and civilian paramilitary forces. Since then the terror has never stopped — tens of thousands more have "disappeared" or been extrajudicially executed

*A young Guatemalan couple at a dance. On the right is Carlos Ernesto Cuevas Molina, a student and trade union leader who "disappeared" in 1984. Witnesses saw him being shot and forced into a car by four heavily armed men believed to be members of the security forces. On the left is his wife, Rosario Godoy de Cuevas, who helped found GAM, the Mutual Support Group for the Appearance of our Relatives Alive, shortly after her husband "disappeared". In March 1985, four days after two GAM leaders were tortured to death, she too was killed along with her brother and three-year-old son: the authorities said they were the victims of a car accident.*
*(c) Jean-Marie Simon*

by the same forces, although the rate has fluctuated with changes of government and there have been recent improvements. Most of the "disappeared", including hundreds of children, have never been seen again. Thousands of mutilated bodies have been found over the years, but few can be identified.

In Peru a pattern of "disappearances" began in 1983 and soon became an almost daily occurrence. Over the past 10 years, Amnesty International has compiled detailed records of over 4,300 victims: the true figure is believed to be far higher.

Mass "disappearances" have also taken place outside Latin America in countries such as Lebanon, Iraq and Sri Lanka. In Iraq, several hundred thousand people are now known to have "disappeared" since 1980. Many are feared to be dead. The victims — men, women and children —include Kurds, Arabs, Turcomans, Assyrians, Sunni Muslims, Shi'a Muslims, Christians, members of prohibited political parties and their families, suspected political opponents, military personnel and deserters, disaffected members of the elite, relatives of deportees, people induced to return home under official amnesties, and more.

Kurds living in Iraq have been particularly targeted. In 1983, for example, some 8,000 male members of the Barzani clan between the ages of eight and 70 were arrested in resettlement camps near Arbil and have not been seen since. One month after their arrest, President Saddam Hussain said in a speech that "those people were severely punished and went to Hell...".

Five years later whole Kurdish families "disappeared" from hundreds of villages after they were rounded up by government forces in an attempt to annihilate, once and for all, the Kurdish identity and way of life. This wave of arrests — known as Operation Anfal — led to the "disappearance" of over 100,000 Kurds, most within a four-month period. It is now known that many of them were killed.

The arrogance of the Iraqi authorities in the way they deal with "disappearances" is particularly shocking. Imagine a scene where government officials tell a family the devastating news that their "disappeared" relative has been secretly executed. They then tell the family that they can only have the body for burial if they pay a fee to cover "state expenses" — including the cost of the bullets used in the execution. Incredibly, such a scene is not uncommon in Iraq.

Most families of the "disappeared" in Iraq, however, are still waiting for news. Few dare to make inquiries for fear of meeting the same fate. In any case, the authorities routinely deny holding the person in question, even when there were eye-witnesses to the arrest.

Good news for some relatives did come during an uprising in March 1991, when many Kurds and Arabs who had "disappeared" in the 1970s and 1980s were found alive. During their brief control of major cities and towns in northern and southern Iraq, opposition forces broke into prisons and detention centres, releasing the inmates.

In Sri Lanka "disappearances" reached catastrophic proportions in the late 1980s and are continuing, although on a lesser scale. The tactic developed soon after the creation of a new police commando unit, the Special Task Force (STF). Young men arrested by this unit, as well as subsequently by the army, began to "disappear" in increasing numbers from the mid-1980s. Testimonies from released prisoners described the torture and killing of many prisoners in STF or army camps, followed by the secret disposal of bodies.

In the northeast, government forces confronting an armed Tamil separatist movement used mass "disappearances" to sow terror and avoid accountability for political killings. Amnesty International recorded 680 "disappearances" between 1984 and mid-1987, when Indian forces took over responsibility for the area. After armed conflict between the Sri Lankan government and the separatists resumed in the northeast in June 1990, the number of newly recorded "disappearances" reached thousands within months. In the south, where the security forces suppressed a rising armed insurgency within the majority Sinhalese community, tens of thousands of people "disappeared" between 1987 and 1990.

As the number of "disappearances" soared in both regions, mutilated bodies, some burned beyond recognition, began appearing by roadsides, in cemeteries or in rivers. Bodies were found smouldering on pyres of rubber tyres. Some might have belonged to people known to have "disappeared", but no one will ever know.

Since early 1992, Amnesty International has recorded "disappearances" in at least 20 countries. The reports include scores of "disappearances" in Indonesia and East Timor; at least 12 in Haiti; scores in India and the Sudan; dozens in Zaire; and at least 16 in the Philippines. Others were recorded in countries such as Papua New Guinea, Senegal and Turkey.

The trend internationally has not, however, been all for the worse. In several countries there has been a dramatic decrease in the number of new "disappearances" in recent years, if not a total eradication of the practice. They include Argentina, Chile, El Salvador, Guatemala, Morocco, Namibia and Zimbabwe (although in some cases, such as Guatemala, other forms of repression have replaced "disappearance").

Yet even in these countries, the suffering caused by "disappearances" has not ended. The families and friends of the "disappeared", in the overwhelming majority of cases, are still waiting for news of their loved ones as governments fail to resolve past "disappearances". The Namibian authorities, for example, have failed to investigate "disappearances" and political killings carried out by both the South African authorities and by the armed opposition South West African People's Organisation which is now in government.

Around the world, the efforts of families and others to find out what happened to the "disappeared" have been obstructed at almost every turn. Their determination and courage, however, will ensure that the "disappeared" and the crimes of past governments will not be forgotten. This was summed up by Gabriela Jiménez, the wife of Eduardo Aníbal Blanco Araya, who "disappeared" in Honduras in 1981, when she declared:

*"There are thousands of cases like ours in the whole of Latin America.... There is the grief of mothers, the hope of wives and the sorrow of children...and we will not give up because we believe in the right to life, the full respect of human rights, justice and peace."*

## Political killings

An indication of the obscene world we live in must surely be the enormous variety of ways government officials devise to murder defenceless people.

Victims are shot dead by hired assassins, blown up by grenades and slaughtered in groups. They are stabbed, strangled, drowned or poisoned. Families are herded into huts and burned alive. Young men are forced into pits and railway carriages and suffocated to death. Women are raped and mutilated before being bayoneted. Prisoners are starved to death or left in stifling dungeons to die of dehydration.

The sites of political killings are just as varied. Prison cells and courtyards, police stations, military barracks and government offices frequently become death chambers. Just as often, people are killed in their homes in front of their families, in busy streets or at bus-stops. Others are shot down near battlefields or in places of worship, schools or hospitals.

Some victims are targeted for assassination, others just happen to be in the wrong place at the wrong time. They may be alleged government opponents or people targeted for their religion, ethnic group, language or colour. They may be people living in an area where the whole population is seen as the enemy, or merely the unfortunate victims of reprisal attacks. They may be people deemed to be "troublemakers" — such as trade unionists, human rights activists, community leaders, lawyers or teachers — or "street children" whose only crime is to be hungry and homeless.

Government responses to political killings are almost as varied as the victims and the ways they are killed. Some killings are denied. Others are justified. Some are covered up. Others are blamed on unofficial forces.

Richard de Zoysa was a brave campaigner for human rights in Sri Lanka. On 19 February 1990 his bloated, naked body was found on a beach, with gunshot wounds in the head and neck. He had been abducted from his home the previous day.

He was known to the authorities as a human rights activist, broadcaster and writer of political satire. One of the six men who abducted him was recognized by his mother as a senior police officer in Colombo: she also said that one of the others had been wearing police uniform. The authorities failed to investigate the killing properly and inquiries were obstructed. All the evidence points to the fact that he was singled out for assassination by government forces.

Such targeted assassinations are perhaps the most blatant type of political killings. Individuals are selected because of their opposition to the government or criticism of its policies, and killers hired by the state are set loose with a hit list.

The very nature of these killings means that it is frequently difficult to determine who actually carried out the assassinations. Governments deny all responsibility, often blaming "death squads" or other forces which they say are acting completely beyond their control. Sometimes the killings are disguised as accidents or the result of random violence. At other times, the bodies are hidden or mutilated to conceal the crime.

Targeted political assassinations are reported around the world. In South Africa, dozens of leading opponents of the *apartheid* system have been gunned down in their homes or on the streets. Middle and high ranking members of the African National Congress (ANC), the South African Communist Party and the trade unions, members of the ANC's military wing and other returned exiles have been, and are still being, assassinated by hit squads composed of elements within the security forces or killers acting with their acquiescence. In Brazil and Guatemala, peasants, trade union leaders and human rights and community activists are routinely singled out.

Some governments do not dispute that their forces were responsible for killings of known political opponents, but they do dispute the circumstances. They may claim, for instance, that the victim or victims died as a result of the security forces meeting armed resistance. Such a scenario is termed an "encounter" killing in India. In May 1990, for example, two Sikh students, Harpal Singh and Baljit Singh, were killed by police in what the authorities said was an "armed encounter" in Kotla Ajner village. But the two men had actually been arrested. Witnesses and journalists refuted the official story. One journalist wrote: "The circumstantial evidence...clearly shows that it was a case of a fake police encounter.... According to villagers, the victims were tortured by the police for a couple of hours and later killed."

The evidence showing that deliberate killings are a matter of policy in some Indian states includes an order issued in August 1989 by the Director General of Police in the Punjab to all district superintendents of police in the state. It included a list of 53 people and specified: "Rewards for the apprehension/liquidation of wanted terrorists/extremists". The Attorney General stated a year later that the order had lapsed. Nevertheless, this and other such messages from the state encouraged police to summarily kill unresisting suspected opponents on the spot or after arrest and attribute the killings to "encounters". In mid-1990, the new Governor of Punjab appealed to police officers to "stop fake encounters". Despite this, the killings continue. In 1992 alone, hundreds of political activists were alleged to have been deliberately killed in incidents falsely described as "encounters" by the police in Punjab, or in "cross-fire" — a term increasingly used to conceal numerous

*Hundreds of "disappearances" and extrajudicial executions have been reported in India in recent years. Here, Mahmood al-Hassan Farooqi shows pictures of his two sons, Tajuddin Mohammed, an engineering student, and 14-year-old Imtiaz Ul-Uddin Ahmad. They were deliberately shot dead in their home by the Border Security Force (BSF) in Jammu and Kashmir state on 31 July 1992, apparently in reprisal for an attack on the BSF. Imtiaz was killed in his mother's arms. (c) Janina Struk*

*Police throwing missiles at anti-government demonstrators during mass protests in the Thai capital, Bangkok, in May 1992. The security forces later fired into the crowds and beat demonstrators to death. At least 52 people were killed and around 700 injured. (c) Popperfoto*

killings in custody of political activists by paramilitary forces and the army in another Indian state, Jammu and Kashmir.

Some political killings are targeted not at specific individuals but at entire communities. These may arise from government operations against ethnic, cultural, racial or religious groups — whether national majorities or minorities — or political movements. Many of the mass political killings recorded in this report fall into this category. They include many of the horrific massacres described in countries such as Bosnia-Herzegovina, Burundi, India, Indonesia, Iraq, Myanmar, Peru and Sri Lanka. Governments may or may not accept responsibility for such killings. Sometimes they attribute them to spontaneous violence spurred by intercommunal hatred or to uncontrollable battles between "extremists of the left and right" from which the government stands aloof. At other times, they claim the actions of their forces were necessary, lawful and justifiable in order to maintain peace and national security. It is only when the truth emerges about the circumstances of the killings that it can be ascertained whether or not they were in fact extrajudicial executions.

Often political killings are carried out simply for revenge, particularly during counter-insurgency operations. Troops may hold communities collectively responsible for attacks on them — or simply lash out at whoever is within their reach. On 17 August 1992, for example, government forces shot dead over 100 unarmed men, women and children in their houses, in streets and in the fields surrounding the town of Doba in southern Chad. The day before a vehicle had failed to stop at a road-block near the town and soldiers opened fire, killing two people. The next morning insurgents supporting the Committee for the Revitalization of Peace and Democracy, an armed group opposed to President Idriss Déby's government, attacked Doba's garrison, but were repelled. Soldiers then went on the rampage in the town, killing unarmed adults and children indiscriminately.

Many political killings are entirely random, resulting from the excessive use of force by security forces when confronting civil unrest or in situations such as ill-conceived crackdowns on crime. The victims are not, by and large, individually targeted. They are killed because they are in the vicinity of protests or because they belong to a community or social class which is seen as a threat to law and order. In these cases, governments often obscure or distort the facts behind the killings while maintaining that the deaths were justifiable under international human rights standards.

Political killings caused by excessive use of force often occur in crowd control situations. A recent example was in Thailand, where security forces killed at least 52 people during four days of demonstrations in May 1992. At least 21 other people went missing and around 700 were injured.

The mass demonstrations in Bangkok, which began in April and involved hundreds of thousands of people, were in protest at the appointment of General Suchinda Khraprayun as Prime Minister. On 17 May, after General Suchinda declared a State of Emergency and banned all gatherings of more than 10 people, the security forces began moving through the streets firing automatic weapons, at first into the air, and then directly into the crowds. For the next three days, the security forces repeated such attacks, often killing people at close range. Other demonstrators were beaten and kicked to death. Reports flew in from around the city of people being gunned down in sidestreets or in buildings where they were hiding.

Many of the 52 known deaths were extrajudicial executions. International standards establish that lethal force should not be used unless strictly unavoidable in order to protect life. In Bangkok, the security forces opened fire on unarmed crowds who were not threatening the lives of either security forces or civilians. Medical evidence indicated that many of the dead had been shot in the back or at point-blank range.

In some cases of apparent extrajudicial executions, the circumstances surrounding the killings are far from clear cut. However, the conduct of the state combined with a pattern of similar incidents often point to the probability that the killings were deliberate and unlawful.

For example, since 1982 Amnesty International has been concerned about dozens of killings carried out in suspicious circumstances by members of the security forces in Northern Ireland (United Kingdom). Serious allegations have been made that there is an official policy to deliberately kill rather than arrest suspected members of armed opposition groups.

These allegations have been strengthened by the government's consistent refusal to mount independent and impartial inquiries into such killings as required by international standards, the result of which is that the full circumstances are not brought to light. The findings of the only detailed internal inquiry, led by a senior police officer from another force, were never published and although the inquiry found evidence of police misconduct, no officers were prosecuted because of "national security" and "public interest" considerations. The authorities' unwillingness to carry out thorough investigations and make the full facts publicly known suggests that there was much they wished to hide.

What all political killings by governments have in common is that they could have been avoided — the victims could have been arrested and could still be alive — and that they serve the perceived interests of the government at some level.

## Background to the terror

Governments resort to political killings and "disappearances" when they believe they will achieve their aims more easily than by using lawful means. They often take the decision during wars or when opposition forces, whether they be non-violent political parties, armed groups or secessionist or nationalist movements, are challenging their power. In a climate of conflict, governments believe they can justify brutal repression in the name of preserving law and order or "national unity", despite using methods which are both unlawful and likely to foment even greater disorder and divisions within the society. Just as often, however, governments turn to such tactics in times of peace to crush opposition. In fact, "disappearances" and political killings are particularly suited to governments wishing to repress opposition in times of nominal peace and normality: both methods are tailored to the evasion of accountability and the maintenance of a facade of legality.

Amnesty International never takes sides in wars, nor does it concern itself with the merits or otherwise of national, regional, cultural, ethnic or other internal conflicts. Its aim is to stop human rights violations by exposing human rights crimes and showing that far from being an "inevitable" consequence of conflict, as many governments claim, they are only committed if the authorities order or tolerate them. Amnesty International's role is constantly to remind governments and public opinion that there are international standards for the protection of human rights, established by governments themselves, which all governments are bound to observe, irrespective of the circumstances.

International law does not outlaw all war, nor killings in wars, but it does aim to restrict the horrors. For example, the four Geneva Conventions of 1949, supplemented by the two Additional Protocols adopted in 1977, provide for the humane treatment of people not involved in the fighting in times of armed conflict.

No government claims it has the right to kill civilians and others who are protected under the Geneva Conventions. Yet almost all wars result in the widespread breaking of the norms of both the Geneva Conventions and human rights laws.

In the Gulf conflict of 1990 to 1991, for example, hundreds of unarmed civilians were extrajudicially executed in Kuwait by Iraqi troops. Victims included children shot in the head at close range whose bodies were then dumped outside their homes. Hundreds of detainees also "disappeared": many remain unaccounted for. Following the withdrawal of Iraqi troops from Kuwait, scores of people were extrajudicially executed by Kuwaiti forces in a wave of revenge killings — murdered for the actions of others. Victims included Palestinian, Iraqi and Sudanese residents in Kuwait who were singled out because of their national identity and shot in public or tortured to

*In the Israeli-Occupied Territories, over 200 Palestinian children aged 16 or under have been killed by Israeli forces since the Palestinian uprising began in late 1987. Eleven-year-old Rana Abu Tuyur was shot dead by Israeli soldiers in Khan Yunes in the Gaza Strip in December 1992. A curfew had just been lifted and she was on her way to collect milk for her family.*

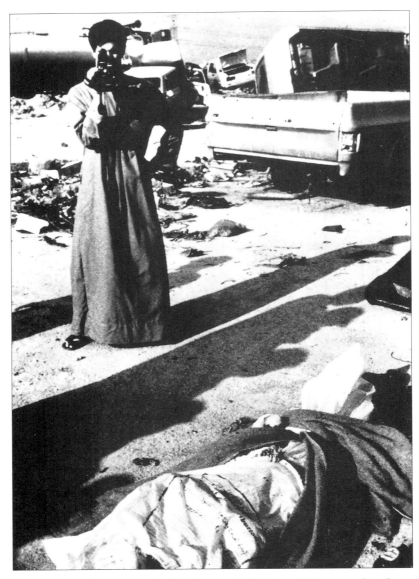

*Scores of people were extrajudicially executed by Kuwaiti forces and civilian vigilantes in a wave of revenge killings following the withdrawal of Iraqi troops from Kuwait in 1991. The picture shows the body of a local television presenter accused of collaborating with Iraqis: he was shot dead before being wrapped in a sack and left on a city rubbish dump.*
*(c) John Reardon/Katz Pictures Ltd*

death in secret. The cases of at least 62 detainees who "disappeared" in custody have been documented.

Populations living under occupation by a foreign power are particularly liable to human rights violations. There is, in addition to more general human rights standards, a separate body of international law designed specifically to regulate the conduct of occupying powers. However, as has been shown in both occupied Kuwait and the Israeli-Occupied Territories, governments do not always respect these international standards. Since 1987 hundreds of Palestinian civilians have been killed by Israeli forces during the Palestinian uprising — the *intifada* — including apparent victims of extrajudicial executions. In East Timor, illegally occupied by Indonesia since 1975, hundreds of civilians have been killed or "disappeared" by the occupying troops.

One of the most disturbing developments of the 1990s has been the dramatic rise in the number of people slaughtered by governments seeking to suppress ethnic and nationalist movements. In almost all cases, repressive measures have entrenched or exacerbated conflicts and dimmed prospects for dialogue.

Since June 1991 the former federal Yugoslavia has been torn apart by nationalist conflicts. All sides have been guilty of horrendous human rights crimes, although Serbian irregular forces and the Yugoslav National Army (JNA) have perpetrated the greatest number of abuses in both Croatia and Bosnia-Herzegovina (see Chapter 2).

In several countries which were formerly part of the Soviet Union, bitter inter-ethnic disputes continue. In Azerbaydzhan, where armed conflict continues over the disputed region of Nagorno-Karabakh, which is mainly populated by ethnic Armenians, hundreds of non-combatant civilians have been deliberately and arbitrarily killed. In February 1992, for instance, over 100 Azeri non-combatants, including women and children, were said to have been killed by ethnic Armenian paramilitary forces while attempting to leave the scene of fighting around the town of Khodzhali. Two months later, 45 unarmed Armenian inhabitants of Maraga in Nagorno-Karabakh, including children, were reportedly massacred after Azerbaydzhani army units entered the village.

Civil wars, many of them based on nationalist or ethnic conflicts, have been the background to staggering levels of political killings and "disappearances" elsewhere in the world.

In the Sudan, troops and government-backed militia have

killed thousands of men, women and children from southern ethnic groups since the outbreak of civil war in 1983. In mid-1992, for example, following intense fighting between government forces besieged in Juba and the rebel Sudan People's Liberation Army (SPLA), government troops shot dead at least 300 unarmed civilians and prisoners when they regained control of part of Juba. Many other detainees "disappeared". Mass political killings have also been reported in the remote Nuba mountains. Hundreds of civilians were reportedly extrajudicially executed there in late December 1992 and early January 1993.

In Somalia's long and merciless civil war, in which tens of thousands of civilians have been deliberately killed by rival armed forces or died in the fighting or as a result of starvation or disease, gross human rights abuses have been a regular occurrence. Just one example was in April 1992, when General Aideed's faction of the ruling United Somali Congress Party massacred civilians in the town of Bulohawo, near Somalia's border with Kenya. A survivor recalled:

> "Many people had fled from Bulohawo before General Aideed's forces came. Those remaining were mostly old men, women and children. Aideed's soldiers gathered everyone in the town centre and separated people by clan, marking out members of the Darod clan. They killed the Darod men and raped the women. Those who tried to escape were shot or bayoneted. The bodies were burned and the bones left lying there."

Horrendous levels of political killings have also accompanied the armed conflict which has torn Liberia apart in the past three years. In 1990 an estimated 20,000 civilian non-combatants were deliberately killed following the invasion of Liberia in December 1989 by the National Patriotic Front of Liberia (NPFL), a Liberian opposition force headed by Charles Taylor. Mass killings were perpetrated by the NPFL and by the Armed Forces of Liberia (AFL), the government armed force which supported former President Samuel Doe, who was killed in 1990, and which was reinstated in November 1992 as Liberia's national army by the Interim Government of National Unity in Monrovia. Those particularly targeted in the killings were members of the Gio and Mano ethnic groups which were perceived as supporting the NPFL, and the Krahn and Mandingo groups which were identified with former President Doe.

After military forces were sent to Liberia in 1990 by Nigeria and other members of the Economic Community of West African States (ECOWAS), hundreds of Nigerian and other West African civilians resident in Liberia, including children, were taken hostage by the NPFL and many were killed. In mid-August 1992 civilians accused of supporting either the NPFL or the United Liberation Movement for Democracy in Liberia (ULIMO), an armed group mostly comprising supporters of former President Doe, were reportedly killed by both sides as they contested control of Tubmanburg, 60 kilometres north of Monrovia. In September 1992 Charles Taylor acknowledged that NPFL troops were "perpetrating atrocities" and said that he would take "drastic military action" against those responsible. However, widespread human rights abuses continue to be committed by all sides involved in the conflict.

For example, in June 1993 around 500 civilians were killed at Harbel, near Monrovia. The victims had sought refuge in a workers' compound at an abandoned rubber plantation after fleeing areas of armed conflict. Although the NPFL was initially blamed for the massacre, evidence emerged that the AFL may have been responsible. Earlier in the year, in March, ULIMO forces were reported to have summarily executed 14 young men suspected of supporting the NPFL at Zorzor in Lofa County, and to have killed 13 civilians at Haindi, 80 kilometres from Monrovia. AFL members were also responsible for political killings in 1992 and early 1993.

In a largely hidden but nevertheless brutal civil war in neighbouring Sierra Leone, hundreds of prisoners captured in fighting, as well as many others suspected of being rebels or collaborators, have been extrajudicially executed by government forces. In March 1991, an invasion force entered Sierra Leone from the part of Liberia controlled by the NPFL. The invasion force captured areas in the south and east of Sierra Leone, killing hundreds of people who refused to help them. Sierra Leonean government troops sent to oppose the rebels recaptured towns and then were reported to have summarily executed people suspected of joining or assisting the invasion force. Villagers were asked to point out rebels and their supporters. If the suspects could not produce witnesses to vouch for them, they were taken away and shot, often in public. Some suspects were tortured before being killed.

In northern and eastern Uganda, government forces fighting civil wars have deliberately killed hundreds of civilians since the present government took power in 1986. In July 1989, for example,

*One of the thousands of civilians killed in southern Sudan since the outbreak of civil war in 1983. The victim was killed in Bor by the Torit faction of the rebel Sudan People's Liberation Army in late 1991.*

*In Liberia's civil war, mass political killings have been committed by all sides. Most victims have been targeted because of their ethnic origin. Here, a rebel soldier shoots dead a captured member of the Armed Forces of Liberia in Monrovia, July 1990. (c) Reuters/Popperfoto*

69 young men suffocated after soldiers locked them in a railway carriage in Mukura, eastern Uganda, and left them to die.

In Afghanistan, political killings have been widely reported as civil war continues to ravage the country. They have been committed by every group involved in the conflict, including government troops, militia and Mujahideen groups aligned with the government of President Burhanuddin Rabbani (which took power in Kabul in mid-1992) and those opposed to it. The victims have frequently been targeted as members of particular ethnic, religious or political groups, and have in some cases included children.

On 11 February 1993, for instance, members of the Shi'a Muslim minority were attacked in Kabul's Afshar district by government troops, militia and members of the pro-government *Ittehad-e-Islami* group. Several men, all civilians, were killed in front of their families and other violations were committed. A young nurse who witnessed the events said:

> "There were 12 of them. They broke down the door, then made advances towards my sister and me. My father tried to stop them, but they hit him and then tortured him. They cut off one of his feet and both his hands in the courtyard. One of them threw my father's hands to a dog belonging to one of the commanders."

One young woman said she had seen four of her neighbours having their throats cut with bayonets. Another reported that her husband and three daughters had been killed by the attackers in front of her. The attack was apparently in retaliation for earlier killings of members of the Pashtun and Tajik communities.

In several countries government forces have committed gross human rights violations when tensions between different ethnic or national groups have degenerated into intercommunal violence. In these circumstances, the duty of the authorities is to keep the peace. All too often, however, governments themselves have abandoned the rule of law to trample on the human rights of a section of their citizens.

In Burundi tensions between the majority Hutu ethnic group and the Tutsi ethnic minority, which held power until mid-1993, were exacerbated by mass deliberate and arbitrary killings of Hutu civilians by the security forces, which are dominated by Tutsi. Such massacres occurred in 1965, 1969, 1972, 1988 and 1991. In 1972 alone, 80,000 or more civilians were murdered by the security forces. In 1988, at least 5,000 civilians were killed during what the

*Intercommunal violence has often been the background to mass political killings by government forces. The photograph shows members of Burundi's security forces, which are overwhelmingly recruited from the country's Tutsi minority, in August 1988. That year, at least 5,000 people, most of them belonging to the previously politically marginalized majority Hutu ethnic group, were killed during what the government described as counter-insurgency operations. (c) Paul Henry Versele/GAMMA*

government described as a counter-insurgency operation against armed rebels. Some sources estimated that 20,000 were massacred, many as they fled from the advancing troops.

Despite some attempts by the government after 1988 to improve intercommunal relations and human rights, the violations continued. In late 1991, for example, at least 1,000 people, most of them Hutu, were reported to have been extrajudicially executed by government soldiers and dozens "disappeared". In June 1993 a President from the Hutu ethnic group was elected for the first time. It remains to be seen how his government will come to grips with the legacy of past violations.

Government responsibility for intercommunal violence was particularly clear in Kenya in 1992. Over 700 people were killed that year in ethnic clashes in western and central Kenya which were allegedly instigated or condoned by the government. Credible evidence emerged that one group responsible for many of the killings was supported and financed by senior government officials. The group was nicknamed "Kalenjin warriors", Kalenjin being the President's ethnic group.

When armed opposition groups gain control of territory or populations, government forces often resort to political killings and "disappearances" as they fight to maintain order or power. The protection of human rights may be undermined by, or subordinated to, what are seen as the exigencies of national security. Members of the security forces, and others acting with their support, may in these circumstances feel free to kill with impunity.

Armed opposition groups can present governments with particular difficulties in the maintenance of order and political stability. When an armed opposition group threatens the state, perhaps using methods of terror itself, and the government launches a counter-insurgency campaign to combat it, the possibility of violence being inflicted on unarmed or defenceless civilians by the security forces is always present.

Under these circumstances, minimum humane standards applicable to the conduct of both government and insurgent forces can be derived from humanitarian law as set out in Article 3, common to the four Geneva Conventions, which apply to situations of internal armed conflict. These protect all those not taking part in the hostilities, including those who have been captured, surrendered or are wounded or incapacitated in any other way: they prohibit murder, mutilation, cruel treatment, torture, hostage-taking, humiliating or degrading treatment, and summary executions.

Governments are, in addition, bound to respect other binding norms of international law, whatever the circumstances. Even when armed opposition groups are committing gross abuses, these never provide justification for violations by government forces. Apart from the fact that basic human rights should be inviolate at all times, if governments show contempt for them, then others may feel free to do likewise, further generating a cycle of terror.

Yet around the world, governments confronting armed opposition groups have violated these standards on a massive scale. In the Philippines, for example, no section of society has escaped brutal repression during a counter-insurgency campaign that has been waged for decades by very different types of government. When an elected government was formally restored in 1986, the new government of Corazon Aquino promised to make a clean break with the policies and practices of President Marcos' government, whose regime had become a byword for human rights violations. Since then, however, hundreds of unarmed civilians have been killed by government forces, with the authorities continuing to claim that the victims were legitimate targets. The facts tell a different story. Whole families have been gunned down. Villagers working in fields have been shot dead. Women have been raped by gangs of soldiers before being killed. The most inhuman forms of torture, including castration, have been inflicted on people targeted for death. And the victims have frequently been the socially and economically disadvantaged and politically weak, not the insurgents.

Similar violations have taken place in less well-known conflicts. In Djibouti, for instance, where the government faces continuing armed opposition in the north and southwest of the country from the Front for the Restoration of Unity and Democracy (FRUD), dozens of civilians were extrajudicially executed, reportedly by soldiers, in February 1992. Many of the victims appeared to have been killed in reprisal attacks. For example, in Yoboki village in the southwest, some 50 civilians were reportedly extrajudicially executed by government troops after a FRUD force withdrew from the village.

Mass political killings also frequently coincide with violent changes of government, particularly when the new authorities have no mandate from the people and resort to terror to establish their power.

In Haiti, for example, a military coup overthrew the elected government of President Jean-Bertrand Aristide in September 1991. The days following the coup were marked by violent repression, particularly in the poor communities where support for President Aristide was strongest. Soldiers deliberately and indiscriminately fired into crowds, killing hundreds of people, including children. In one neighbourhood soldiers reportedly raided private homes and shot dead more than 30 unarmed people. They then forced relatives and other local people to bury the bodies. Since then, hundreds of other people have been extrajudicially executed, particularly President Aristide's political supporters and those living in the poorer districts of Port-au-Prince where popular protests against the new government have been common.

In some countries, extrajudicial executions are carried out under the cover of "anti-crime" operations. In Indonesia, for example, more than 30 "criminal suspects" were arbitrarily shot dead by police in 1992 as part of a continuing "shoot-on-sight" policy instituted by the police in Jakarta in 1989. Similar killings during "anti-crime" operations have also been reported in Pakistan and Venezuela.

Governments face challenges not entirely of their own making: opposition movements, high crime levels, determined non-violent advocates of political change, intercommunal tensions. But whatever the circumstances, political killings and "disappearances" can never be justified, and will never provide a long-term solution to the problems. It may take decades, but governments who kill their own citizens will one day pay the price of their own cruelty.

## Who carries out the terror?

*"Martial law is neither more nor less than the will of the general who commands the army; in fact, martial law means no law at all."*

Major General Khin Nyunt, Secretary-1 of the State Law and Order Restoration Council and head of military intelligence in Myanmar, May 1991.

The military government in Myanmar apparently feels little shame about the way its troops systematically violate human rights. From the day it seized power in September 1988, in the name of the State Law and Order Restoration Council (SLORC), its forces have ruthlessly and openly suppressed virtually all expressions of dissent.

Within days of taking power, soldiers had shot dead at least a thousand unarmed demonstrators taking part in nationwide protests against one-party military rule. Since then, particularly following the SLORC's refusal to hand over power to the National League for Democracy, which won general elections in 1990, official security forces have continued to commit gross human rights violations with impunity.

Widespread extrajudicial executions have been accompanied by reports of systematic torture, rape and ill-treatment by security force personnel. Hundreds of thousands of people, including villagers abducted by the military and prisoners serving sentences for criminal offences, have been forced to work as porters for the military. Many have died of exhaustion or severe ill-treatment, including children and pregnant women. Others have been shot dead when they proved physically incapable of continuing, for disobeying orders or for attempting an escape. Still others have been killed when trying to evade conscription for portering.

Most of the victims belong to one of Myanmar's several ethnic minorities. Particularly targeted have been Muslims in Rakhine State: by July 1992 over a quarter of a million of them had fled to Bangladesh, fearing for their lives.

A witness described one of the many political killings of alleged supporters of insurgent groups. The victim was 30-year-old Abdul Rahman from a village in Buthidaung township.

*"One day he was sitting outside his house when the MI-18 (Military Intelligence agents) came and shot him. They just shot him there, in the street. They said that he was an...insurgent, but he was just an ordinary farmer."*

Many other political killings in Myanmar have taken place during counter-insurgency operations. Part of the army strategy involves declaring large areas to be "free-fire" zones: ethnic minority communities are forced to move to "strategic hamlets" under strict curfews and rigid controls. During these operations, the army arbitrarily kills civilians, rapes and otherwise tortures villagers during interrogation, and makes mass arrests. In some areas the army has designated all the villages as "black", meaning that anyone found there can be shot on sight.

The SLORC has consistently denied responsibility for human rights violations and ignores the copious evidence of atrocities committed by its forces. It has attempted to justify its use of martial law as "protecting the state from disintegration" and has claimed that this task has "nothing to do with human rights". Amnesty International knows of not a single case in which military or police personnel responsible for political killings or other serious human rights violations have been brought to justice.

Gross human rights violations by police, army and other officials openly employed by the state are common in several other countries where the government makes little pretence of being accountable to its citizens. They include those in China and Iraq.

Elsewhere, governments have organized or encouraged "death squads" or paramilitary organizations to continue the same repressive operations at one remove.

A former Salvadorian soldier explains how it works:

*"Early in 1980 I volunteered to join what is referred to in El Salvador as a death squad. However, in my experience the death squad has no independent existence outside the Salvadorian military and security forces. It is simply a form of duty which the military personnel are ordered to carry*

*The security forces in Myanmar systematically violate human rights with impunity. Widespread political killings have been accompanied by reports of torture, rape and ill-treatment. Hundreds of thousands of people have been seized by the military and forced to serve as porters. Many have died from exhaustion; others have been shot or beaten to death. The picture shows the body of a porter, hands tied behind the back, floating in the Thanlwin river in 1992. (c) Ben Bohane*

*Members of the Alsa Masa "vigilante" group in Davao City. Hundreds of political killings have been carried out in the Philippines since 1987 by semi-official "vigilante" groups and the official militia, the Citizen Armed Force Geographical Unit.*

*out while not in uniform. Within the military, these operations are not referred to as 'death squads' but simply as 'missions'.*

A "death squad" can be a squad of specialists or any force of regular troops, police or paramilitaries which carries out political killings to order. In some places, the "death squads" do not really exist: killings committed by conventional units of police and army are blamed by the authorities on shadowy forces to deflect attention away from official responsibility. These supposedly untraceable groups are generally identified only by name or area of operation. Their often dramatic names — White Hand, Death to Kidnappers, Secret Army, Black Cats — are intended, apparently, to hide the fact that they are not independent entities as well as to give an added dimension to the terror.

Both military and civilian governments have opted for "death squad" operations as a "quick-fix" solution to a political problem. But once governments have turned to murdering their citizens, the tactic rarely turns out to be short-term.

The security forces in Argentina first started using "death squads" in late 1973. By the time military rule ended in 1983, some 1,500 people had been killed by "death squads" and over 9,000 people had "disappeared", according to the officially appointed National Commission on Disappeared People (CONADEP).

Elsewhere, "death squad" killings continue to haunt the population. In Colombia, clandestine military units operating as named "death squads" first appeared in 1978. Throughout the 1980s the yearly rate of political killings continued to rise, reaching a peak of 3,500 in 1988. Since then, an average of 1,500 people a year have been murdered by covert forces acting in the name of "death squads". Over 1,500 civilians are also believed to have "disappeared" since 1978.

The Colombian authorities have consistently described "death squads" as civilian vigilantes over whom they have no control. Overwhelming evidence shows that this is far from the truth. For example, military spokesmen claimed that a "death squad" known as *Muerte a Secuestradores* (MAS), Death to Kidnappers, which was responsible for killings throughout the country by 1982, was an independent group created by the criminal underworld to combat left-wing guerrillas. However, an investigation by the Colombian Procurator General in 1983 found that 59 serving members of the armed forces had been actively involved in incidents attributed to the MAS. In a report to Congress in 1986, the Procurator General said that military officers used the MAS to "do unofficially what cannot be done officially".

The "death squad" phenomenon often coincides with political killings by readily identifiable paramilitary organizations of armed civilians under varying degrees of governmental control. These forces act on the authority of the government and in concert with conventional police and military forces. Yet governments deny responsibility for the actions of their paramilitary supporters just as they do for those of "death squads".

In the Philippines the government has, since 1987, authorized and encouraged a network of semi-official paramilitaries as part of its counter-insurgency drive. These forces are poorly trained and disciplined, and are encouraged by the police and military authorities to act outside the law in the name of "national security". Unofficial "vigilante" groups have also been allowed to operate. Both have been responsible for many of the hundreds of political killings reported in recent years.

The Citizen Armed Force Geographical Unit (CAFGU), which is thought to have committed numerous extrajudicial killings, was established in 1987 under a constitutional provision allowing for a "citizen armed force". In practice, many members were recruited from the Civilian Home Defense Force (CHDF), which had been widely accused of responsibility for human rights violations under President Marcos and which was supposed to have been disbanded under a presidential order in 1987. The CAFGU is officially supplied and trained by the military and in theory is accountable to it.

The Philippines government also authorized in 1987 the formation of Civilian Self Defense Organizations (CVOs) — ostensibly neighbourhood groups set up to defend local communities. These too have been implicated in political killings and other violations. "Vigilante" groups, such as *Alsa Masa* (Masses Arise), a highly politicized anti-communist organization known to have been responsible for widespread human rights abuses, have operated under the CVO structure. Despite a constitutional provision prohibiting unofficial armed groups, the military has used both CVOs and "vigilante" groups in counter-insurgency operations.

Elsewhere in the world, governments hire individual civilians to do their dirty work. In Turkey, for example, a remarkable taped conversation corroborated widespread claims that the security forces were inciting and recruiting local people to carry out political killings of Kurdish oppositionists.

In early 1992, 16-year-old Rifat Akis was detained on suspicion of membership of the Kurdish Workers' Party (PKK). He claimed that a captain (the commander of a local Gendarmerie Post) forced him to agree under threat to assassinate a leading member of the Social Democratic Populist Party and supplied him with a gun and hand grenades. Rifat Akis' family appealed to members of parliament, who then took him to Ankara Police Headquarters where a conversation between Rifat Akis and the captain was recorded. A section was published in a Turkish newspaper:

"**Rifat Akis**: Hello, this is Rambo Stes [his codename]

**Captain**: Where are you?

**Rifat Akis**: I am in Diyarbakir. I found the man. I'll get rid of him.

**Captain**: Do not speak too openly on the telephone. Get rid of him and come here, your 20 million [around £2,000] is ready.

**Rifat Akis**: How shall I do it?

**Captain**: Pull the fuse on the grenade and throw it at him. Shoot him in the head no more than three times. Do not worry, we have arranged everything. We'll say terrorists killed him."

The captain is still at liberty and on duty. It appears that no legal proceedings have been taken against him.

## Abuses by armed political groups

Two young men — David Ober and Alfred Ojoli — were returning home one evening in May 1991 after washing at a well near their home in northern Uganda. They were seized by a group of armed soldiers, who then hacked off their right hands.

The soldiers who mutilated them were not in the pay of the government. They were members of a rebel force, the United Democratic Christian Army. The rebels accused the two men of being members of a pro-government militia, the "Arrow Brigade". David Ober said: "Although we were not even armed, the rebels decided to cut off our right hands so we can no longer shoot the arrow."

For victims of abuses like these, the pain and suffering are the same, regardless of whether state officials or opposition leaders are behind the crime.

Many governments point to such "terrorist acts" by armed opposition groups to excuse their use of violence against their own people.

For example, Sri Lanka's Presidential Adviser on International Affairs told Amnesty International in 1990:

> *"Predictably, when security forces have to deal with terrorist groups, who, as a matter of ideology and deliberate strategy adopt practices of the most unimaginable savagery, excesses are bound to occur."*

Undoubtedly, armed political groups have committed sickening atrocities. They have tortured, raped and mutilated unarmed civilians. They have deliberately and arbitrarily killed people who offered no threat to them and were not part of the state's repressive machinery. They have taken innocent bystanders hostage — sometimes to exchange for concessions, sometimes to kill, later, when it suited their purpose.

Such crimes should be stopped, and those responsible should be brought to justice. But they can never justify state murder or "disappearances."

In the Indonesian province of Aceh, an armed group called *Aceh Merdeka* has been fighting for independence since the mid-1970s. Since the re-emergence of armed conflict in 1989, its members have committed human rights abuses, including arbitrarily killing civilians they alleged were informers. Amnesty International, which condemns such killings unreservedly, called on the leaders of *Aceh Merdeka* to ensure that all its members abide by the basic standards of international humanitarian law.

The Indonesian government's response to the activities of *Aceh Merdeka* was violent and brutal. Thousands of troops were sent to the area, including elite counter-insurgency units. Devastating attacks on villages and cold-blooded murder became commonplace, resulting in some two thousand civilian deaths in Aceh. Some people were publicly executed, while hundreds of others "disappeared" and were killed secretly, the decomposing and often mutilated bodies of some left in public places as a warning to others.

Commenting on the public display of corpses, a military officer in Aceh said: "Okay, that does happen. But the rebels use terrorist strategies so we are forced to use anti-terrorist strategies."

The cycle of violence will never be broken as long as "anti-terrorist strategies" is a euphemism for summary executions and other abuse of power.

For many years, Amnesty International's main approach to abuses by opposition groups was to report, while addressing only governments. While the organization condemned torture or killing of prisoners by anyone, including opposition groups, it addressed its concerns to governments. Over the years, however, particularly as secessionist and nationalist conflicts proliferated, Amnesty International recognized that it could play a more active role in opposing the widespread and serious problem of abuses by armed political opposition groups and *de facto* authorities. In 1991 the movement decided to widen the scope of its mandate.

Amnesty International policy now is to oppose hostage-taking, torture, the killing of prisoners and other deliberate and arbitrary killings by armed political groups: deliberate killings of civilians who offer no immediate threat are always arbitrary, as are killings of soldiers who have been captured, laid down their arms or been incapacitated. Even in times of war, the principles which regulate the use of force prohibit such actions.

Amnesty International's change of policy has meant increased action to protect individuals in the face of abuses by armed political groups. The object is to influence such groups on behalf of victims, while maintaining Amnesty International's traditional focus on holding governments accountable in line with their international obligations.

Deliberate and arbitrary killings and hostage-taking by political opposition groups are a worldwide phenomenon.

In Africa, long-running insurgencies and civil wars, some of them with major international dimensions, have racked many countries and armed opposition organizations have often treated civilians as a legitimate target. In Mozambique, for example, armed units of the *Resistência Nacional Moçambicana* (RENAMO), Mozambique National Resistance, have murdered and mutilated prisoners and attacked civilians for nearly two decades. The leadership of RENAMO has consistently refused to acknowledge these abuses or to take action to halt them.

In Sudan, the rebel Sudan People's Liberation Army (SPLA) holds large parts of the south of the country, particularly the rural areas. Internal divisions within the SPLA have led to growing violence against non-combatants by SPLA soldiers. The SPLA split in two in August 1991: the breakaway faction is known as the Nasir group and the forces loyal to leader John Garang de Mabior as the Torit group. In September 1992 another faction, known as the Unity group, began operating. Fighting between the various factions has displaced tens of thousands of southern Sudanese civilians and both the Torit and Nasir factions have been responsible for serious abuses of human rights.

In late 1991 Nasir group forces raided Dinka villages in the Bor and Kongor areas, deliberately killing hundreds of civilians. A number of women and children were reportedly abducted. In May 1992 Torit group forces slaughtered members of the Toposa ethnic group living in villages around the town of Kapoeta. Toposa members of a pro-government militia had been involved in the capture of Kapoeta and subsequent attacks on people trying to flee. In September 1992 SPLA soldiers deliberately killed three foreign aid workers and a journalist. The Torit group blamed Unity group troops but subsequent investigations suggested that their own forces were responsible. In April 1993 Torit group forces attacked Nuer villages and feeding centres apparently in reprisal for the massacre of Dinka civilians in late 1991. Hundreds of civilians, many of them helpless victims of famine, were killed.

In South Africa, the continent's last white minority regime continues to imprison, torture and kill its opponents despite moves towards a political settlement. However, the opposition ANC was itself found responsible for torture, ill-treatment and executions in its detention camps over a 12-year period in the late 1970s and 1980s. Many of the victims were members of the ANC's military wing who had opposed aspects of ANC policy. The abuses took place in several African countries, notably Angola, Zambia, Tanzania and Uganda — sometimes with the active collaboration of the government concerned. Following an ANC inquiry, ANC President Nelson Mandela accepted the organization's full responsibility for the abuses.

In the Americas, several armed opposition groups persistently use methods including the deliberate killing of civilians, summary executions and taking hostages.

In May 1980, barely two months before the installation of a civilian government in Peru after more than a decade of military rule, the armed opposition *Partido Comunista del Perú (Sendero Luminoso)*(PCP), Communist Party of Peru (Shining Path), carried out its first assault. The attack heralded a campaign which has been sustained over the past 13 years. In 1984 a second opposition group, the *Movimiento Revolucionario Túpac Amaru* (MRTA), Túpac Amaru Revolutionary Movement, also launched an armed campaign against the state in which it has committed grave human rights abuses.

Since the launch of these campaigns and of the government's counter-insurgency operations, political violence has spread throughout most of Peru. Accurate information about the total number of people killed is not available. However, statistics gathered by credible sources put the number of victims at over 25,000 and suggest that 45 per cent were killed by the PCP, one per cent by the MRTA and 53 per cent by the government's security forces. A high proportion of both government and opposition killings were deliberate and arbitrary: murder by any other name.

In its campaign to overthrow the Peruvian state, the PCP has adopted a variety of strategies. For over a decade it has demanded boycotts of municipal, parliamentary and presidential elections and has threatened and murdered candidates and voters alike. It has summarily killed hundreds of municipal election candidates, mayors and other local and regional state officials and administrators.

The PCP has also deliberately killed members of non-governmental human rights organizations; journalists; priests, nuns and others attached to the Roman Catholic and evangelical churches; political activists from across the political spectrum; and leaders of popular organizations not in sympathy with the PCP's aims and methods. In addition, the organization has summarily killed thousands of peasants accused of collaborating with the counter-insurgency forces or who refused to support the PCP.

Just one example of the PCP's methods shows its disregard for human life. On the night of 10 October 1992 a PCP unit attacked the community of Huayllao, Tambo district in Ayacucho department. Fourteen children aged between four and 15 were among the 47 peasants massacred. The Mayor of Tambo described the incident as "one of the most horrible massacres that has afflicted our department...it was an unspeakable and savage attack in which the elderly, children and defenceless women were killed."

The PCP is unashamed by such acts, it seems. An internal document written in 1991 stated: "...[the PCP's] position is quite clear, we reject and condemn human rights because they are reactionary, counter-revolutionary, bourgeois rights; they are presently the weapon of revisionists and imperialists, principally of yankee imperialism." However, the PCP has specifically cited a range of international human rights and humanitarian standards in its campaign on behalf of its own members imprisoned by the Peruvian government.

In Colombia, guerrilla organizations such as the *Fuerzas Armadas Revolucionarias de Colombia* (FARC), Revolutionary Armed Forces of Colombia, and the *Ejército de Liberación Nacional* (ELN), National Liberation Army, have carried out numerous attacks in which civilians have been deliberately killed. Scores of people have been kidnapped and held to ransom: some have been killed in captivity. Others, including journalists and local government officials, have been taken hostage by guerrilla forces and sometimes held for prolonged periods before being released, often forced to carry messages to the government about proposed negotiations. Other public officials have been seized and held until the Colombian authorities complied with guerrilla demands to investigate the hostages' alleged corrupt practices.

Armed opposition groups in Asia and the Pacific, too, have taken hostages and deliberately targeted and killed unarmed civilians.

In India, such groups have committed numerous human rights abuses in many states, including Jammu and Kashmir, Punjab and Andhra Pradesh. In Punjab, armed separatists have deliberately killed thousands of civilians. They have dragged Hindus from trains and then massacred them. In Jammu and Kashmir, armed separatist groups have captured and killed civilians, taken hostages, tortured prisoners and raped women in their custody. In Andhra Pradesh, they have killed or mutilated alleged "informers".

In Sri Lanka, violence by armed opposition groups has intensified over the years in the face of savage government repression. In the late 1970s and early 1980s, Tamil militants of the Liberation Tigers of Tamil Eelam (LTTE), seeking independence for the northeast of Sri Lanka, attacked mainly state targets. More generalized attacks against civilian targets, such as bombing bus stops and attacking Sinhalese and Muslim communities, came later.

Today the LTTE has excluded almost all expression of dissent within the area it controls by using violent repressive measures against rival groups.

LTTE forces have committed numerous gross abuses of human rights including the massacre of hundreds of non-combatant

Muslim and Sinhalese civilians in attacks on their communities and in attacks on buses and trains. They have tortured and killed prisoners, and abducted people for ransom. They have also executed prisoners whom they accused of being traitors.

A witness described the public execution of alleged informers on the morning of 6 July 1992. A group of LTTE soldiers brought 10 prisoners, including two women, to the road junction at Paranathal. A large crowd of people were forced to watch the proceedings. The prisoners were taken down from the vehicle and told to stand on the sandbags which had been placed ready "so that their blood would not stain the soil". They were told to admit to giving information to the army. When two of them said they had confessed falsely because they had been beaten during interrogation, a member of the LTTE ordered the shooting to start. The 10 were shot in the back. An LTTE member then cut off the head of one of the executed prisoners, who the witness identified as a lorry driver called Nagarajah. The head was put in a box and a woman traveller was forced to take it to the sentry point at the Vavuniya army camp.

Opposition abuses have claimed the lives of ordinary people in many other Asian countries, such as Afghanistan, Bangladesh, Cambodia, Papua New Guinea and the Philippines. In Cambodia, for instance, human rights abuses by the Khmer Rouge threatened the May 1993 UN-monitored elections. In the event, the elections took place with limited disruption, but grave fears remain for Cambodia's prospects.

The fall of the Berlin Wall in 1989 raised hopes for improved respect for human rights in much of Europe. The reality has been an upsurge in ethnic and nationalist conflicts, degenerating in many countries into outright civil war. Widespread human rights abuses have taken place not only in the former Yugoslavia, but, less well publicized, in several republics of the former Soviet Union.

For example, in Tadzhikistan a civil war little reported outside the region between government forces and those supporting an opposition coalition has left up to 20,000 dead, according to official estimates, and displaced over 600,000 people, more than a tenth of the population. Appalling human rights violations took place in the country's capital, Dushanbe, in the weeks after the city was retaken by government forces in December 1992. Equally serious abuses have been reported by all sides in the conflict in other areas, but so far these have been largely impossible to confirm.

Human rights abuses by armed political groups in other

European countries have been going on for many years. In the United Kingdom (UK), members of the Irish Republican Army (IRA) have killed civilians in Northern Ireland and Britain, and have killed captive suspected informants. Other abuses have been committed in Northern Ireland by Protestant groups such as the Ulster Volunteer Force (UVF) and the Ulster Defence Association (UDA). They have killed members of the minority Catholic community in random attacks they said were "reprisals" for IRA violence, as well as suspected informants. In Spain, members of the Basque separatist organization *Euskadi Ta Askatasuna* (ETA), Basque Homeland and Liberty, have deliberately killed civilians as well as members of the security forces in attacks.

In Turkey, during 1992 alone, the Kurdish Workers' Party (PKK) carried out more than a hundred "executions" of prisoners — including teachers, members of the government-organized village guard corps, and people suspected of being police informers. According to reports, in October 1992 PKK guerrillas entered the village of Cevizdali, Bitlis Province, and disarmed the village guards. Shortly afterwards, a small group of guerrillas on the far side of the village exchanged fire with reinforcements from a nearby security post. At the sound of gunshots, the main party of guerrillas reportedly opened fire on the assembled villagers, killing 37 people, including children. Members of the organization *Devrimci Sol*, Revolutionary Left, have also killed several of their own members who were suspected of being informers.

In the Middle East, in countries such as Algeria and Egypt, killings of police and civilians by militant Islamic groups have coincided with drastic clampdowns by the government and a sharp deterioration in respect for human rights. Some victims have been targeted by opposition groups solely on account of their views. In Egypt, for example, Farag Foda, a writer and vocal opponent of Islamic militant groups, was shot dead by two men in June 1992: responsibility for the killing was claimed by the opposition group *Al-Gama'a al-Islamiya*. The writer's 15-year-old son was wounded in the attack.

In Lebanon various militia have for years held people hostage and committed deliberate and arbitrary killings. The lives of thousands of ordinary Lebanese and other Arab nationals have been disrupted or destroyed, although international attention in recent years has focused on the fate of Western hostages.

In the Israeli-Occupied Territories, Palestinians — including members of armed political groups — have killed hundreds of people in recent years. From January to May 1993, Palestinians killed up to 14 Israeli civilians and about 50 Palestinians, many of them suspected of "collaborating" with the Israeli authorities. Some of the victims were interrogated and tortured before being put to death. Palestinian leaders, including leaders of the Palestine Liberation Organization (PLO), have condemned the torture and wanton killing of suspected "collaborators", and have issued charters setting out rules of behaviour in the Occupied Territories. However, Palestinian leaders seem generally to have endorsed the view that "collaborators" may be punished with death if such punishment is approved in a particular case by the top leadership.

In Iraq, human rights abuses have been committed by opponents of the Iraqi government, notably in northern Iraq in areas under the control of the Iraqi Kurdistan Front (IKF) and, since July 1992, the Council of Ministers for the Kurdistan Region. Abuses include torture and ill-treatment of prisoners, the imposition of the death penalty after unfair trials, and other deliberate and arbitrary killings. In October 1991, for example, armed Kurdish units (*Pesh Merga*) summarily executed about 60 unarmed Iraqi soldiers in Sulaimaniya following attacks on residential areas by Iraqi government forces. An IKF investigation into the killings identified 14 Kurds as the suspected perpetrators, most of whom were affiliated to Kurdish political organizations. However, the suspects were released in 1992 after the IKF decided not to pursue the investigation.

Armed opposition groups vary enormously. Some have achieved international sympathy and support and stand on the brink of becoming governments. Others have a mere handful of poorly armed cadres and only popular support or their ability to maintain themselves in remote parts of the country prevents them from being eliminated.

Amnesty International is impartial in its approach to all such groups, as reflected in its determinedly neutral terminology. Organizations referred to as "terrorists" by governments and as "freedom fighters" by supporters are always termed "armed opposition groups" by Amnesty International.

Amnesty International never comments on the legitimacy or illegitimacy of rebellion. It does not oppose the use of force *per se* by opposition groups, only the abuse of human rights. It does not say that political goals can never justify violence.

*Local people stand over the bodies of Iraqi government troops summarily executed by Kurdish forces in Sulaimaniyah in October 1991. An estimated 60 Iraqi soldiers were killed after surrendering.(c) Popperfoto/Reuters*

*A Cambodian woman recovers from a Khmer Rouge attack on a train in July 1990 in which 26 passengers were believed to have been captured or murdered. (c) David Pearson*

But it is passionately concerned about the victims who, despite taking no part in the conflict, are held as hostages, tortured or killed.

No-one — regardless of the provocation — has the right to use torture on another human being. No-one — whether government soldier or rebel — has the right to commit murder. The basic standards of international humanitarian law are the bottom line. If these minimum standards are breached, there is no hope of achieving justice or peace.

# 2

## The victims

### Government critics and opponents

There is no place on earth where a government enjoys universal acclaim from its people. Opposition to authority can never be eradicated. Yet some governments have tried to do precisely that — wipe out all dissent using any means at their disposal.

Recent Iraqi history is a grim testament to such an attempt. Hundreds of thousands of people have been murdered by government forces. Many were targeted simply for belonging to a community that was seen to be opposed to the government.

The killing of an estimated 5,000 men, women and children by chemical weapons in the Kurdish town of Halabja in March 1988 was just one example of mass extermination, made notorious only because journalists could reach the border town from neighbouring Iran. Many other Halabja-style killings are now coming to light.

Over the years, Iraqi forces have developed a myriad of gruesome ways to carry out political killings. Methods used include mass executions by firing-squads, burying victims alive, drowning people in rivers, poisoning, bleeding prisoners to death, "accidental deaths" in helicopters or cars, targeted assassinations, and chemical weapons. Thousands of people have died in custody in mysterious circumstances or as a result of torture.

These killings have been difficult to investigate in the past. The law does not intervene, there has been little access to the country, and the fear pervading every level of society has prevented people speaking out.

Information is now coming out in greater quantities. One source is video footage: Iraqi intelligence and security personnel recorded for posterity many of the atrocities

*The bodies of three victims bear horrific testimony to a policy of mass extermination of Kurds carried out by the Iraqi government in recent years. An estimated 5,000 men, women and children were killed by chemical weapons in this one attack on the Kurdish town of Halabja in 1988. Hundreds of thousands of Kurdish civilians have "disappeared" or been slaughtered since the mid-1980s.*

they committed. Another is the discovery of mass graves in northern Iraq.

Despite this, it is still difficult to assess the extent of political killings, both past and present, of suspected government opponents. In early 1992, for example, President Hussain said that Shi'a Muslims who had participated in the March 1991 uprising in the south (during which thousands of civilians were butchered by government forces) should be machine-gunned for treason. Following this order, repeated and deliberate attacks were launched on civilian targets in the marshes region, but the number of casualties is not known.

What is known is that almost every expression of opposition to the government is met with chilling retribution. Lawyers and members of other professional organizations as well as armed opposition groups and whole communities have all been targeted for murder by the security forces. Even opponents abroad have not been safe.

In many parts of Latin America, critics or opponents of the government or the people and communities presumed, rightly or wrongly, to be their sympathizers, live under a shadow of fear of being targeted for "disappearance" or assassination.

In Peru those at risk even include children. For example, in August 1985 troops armed with knives, submachine guns, rifles and hand grenades entered the village of Accomarca, Ayacucho department, and killed 69 peasants. Among the dead were, according to some reports, 21 children under the age of five, and 10 who were between five and 10 years old. The Ayacucho army commander said that all those who died were guerrillas killed in armed clashes.

The report of the senate commission of inquiry into the incident concluded that the army patrol had attacked and killed defenceless peasants. It cited an interview with Sub-Lieutenant Telmo Hurtado, who asserted that even children were "dangerous" because the PCP began indoctrination "from age two, three, four years old...small children have told about all the things they have to do, so that little by little, by tricks and punishments, they win them to their cause".

In southeast Turkey, allegations of extrajudicial executions of government opponents have become alarmingly common in the past two years. In fact, a pattern has emerged of the systematic elimination of people who are believed to be in contact with the PKK, of people engaged in work on behalf of the Kurdish minority, and of human rights monitors.

Vedat Aydin, President of the Diyarbakir branch of the People's Labour Party (HEP) and a board member of the Turkish Human Rights Association, was abducted from his home on 5 July 1991 by several armed men: witnesses said he had recognized the men and they had identified themselves as police officers. His body was found three days later on a roadside. He had been shot eight times, his arms and legs had been broken and his skull crushed. Initially, the body was quickly buried by the police as "unidentifiable" without a full autopsy being carried out. The perfunctory investigation of the killing as well as aspects of the crime itself suggest that the security forces were responsible.

In the 18 months after Vedat Aydin's murder 42 other officials and members of the HEP were killed in attacks, most of which occurred after the party won a number of parliamentary seats in the general election of October 1991. Other government opponents were also targeted, with a total of over 250 such urban killings recorded in 1992.

Government critics or opponents are targeted for assassination or "disappearance" in several other countries. Mudhar al-Jundi, for example, a 35-year-old engineer and father of a young daughter, has not been heard of since his arrest in Syria in 1987. Like hundreds of others arrested at that time, he was detained for his alleged membership of the Party for Communist Action. His wife, Munira Hawija, was also arrested but subsequently released. Numerous inquiries into Mudhar's whereabouts have been greeted by a wall of silence. Some unofficial sources say he died under torture soon after arrest. Others say he is in Tadmur Prison. The truth is known only to the Syrian authorities.

Duong Nigieb, a member of the Buddhist Liberal Democratic Party (BLDP) in Kompong Som in southern Cambodia, was killed on 19 August 1992 when five gunmen entered his house and shot him twice at close range in the neck and head. Two months earlier State of Cambodia (SOC) authorities had sacked him as an SOC official allegedly because of his affiliation with the BLDP. Local SOC police investigating his death said the motive for the killing was personal, but independent sources named two SOC police officers as responsible.

Hlalanathi "Professor" Sibankulu, a 28-year-old South African trade union organizer and former political detainee, was driving in his car with his sister in November 1992 after attending a trade union workshop in Newcastle, northern Natal. Suddenly they were fired on by people in a car that had been chasing them. They raced to the KwaZulu police station in Madadeni township and begged for help. They pointed to the attackers, who could be seen from the station. The police responded by searching Hlalanathi's car for weapons, of which they found none.

They left the station in disgust. Hlalanathi dropped his sister off and a few hours later he was murdered. The next morning his body was found in his burned-out car. He had been shot in the head. Evidence indicates that the men who chased and shot at Hlalanathi's car were members of the KwaZulu police. This, together with their refusal to assist him at the police station, creates the suspicion that they were directly involved in his murder later that night.

In Papua New Guinea, dozens of supporters of the Bougainville Revolutionary Army, a secessionist group in Bougainville, were extrajudicially executed in 1992. In one incident in May, the day after anniversary celebrations marking a 1990 declaration

*The final moments of Izzet Kezer, a Turkish journalist. He and 11 other journalists were sheltering in the courtyard of a house in Cizre, southeast Turkey, on 23 March 1992 after being fired on from a military vehicle. The journalists held up white flags before walking out towards the vehicle. When they emerged, Izzet Kezer was killed instantly by a burst of gunfire. The rate of alleged extrajudicial executions in the southeast rose dramatically in 1992: the victims included several other journalists, human rights activists and government opponents, particularly those associated with Turkey's Kurdish minority.*

of Bougainville's independence from Papua New Guinea, government troops reportedly entered Okogupa village in Aita and fired indiscriminately, killing at least 17 people. Among the dead were the village chief, his wife and five children.

These cases give a small indication of how frequently governments choose to murder their opponents rather than allow them free speech, negotiate with them, or even, if the tide of opposition is overwhelming, concede to pressure for change. But however brutal their methods, and however successful they are in the short term, history shows that the voice of resistance will never be silenced for good.

## People who defend human rights

Heavily armed men burst into 23-year-old María Rumalda Camey's house early one morning in August 1989. She was dragged screaming from her husband and two small children. They have never seen her again.

No one doubts why she was added to the toll of victims who have "disappeared" or been assassinated by Guatemala's security forces. She was one of the many brave women who defy the terror by refusing to forget past violations by the country's security forces.

María joined the Mutual Support Group for the Appearance of our Relatives Alive (GAM) after her brother-in-law, José Carlos Chitay Nech, "disappeared" in 1985. She knew only too well the risks — five members of her family have "disappeared" or been killed by the security forces.

In February 1993 Chris Batan and two friends were travelling by road to Betwagan, in the Philippine's Mountain Province of northern Luzon, where he was going to investigate past human rights violations. As they approached Betwagan, six armed members of a government militia, the CAFGU, opened fire on him and his two companions. Chris was hit in the leg and fell to the ground. The gunmen approached and shot him in the chest. They then fled after threatening his colleagues, who were able to identify one of the attackers by name.

Chris Batan was undoubtedly killed because of his efforts to protect human rights. He had spent most of his adult life campaigning for the rights of indigenous peoples and worked for Task Force Detainees of the Philippines, a national human rights organization. Friends describe him as "one of the youngest martyrs of the indigenous peoples of the Cordillera".

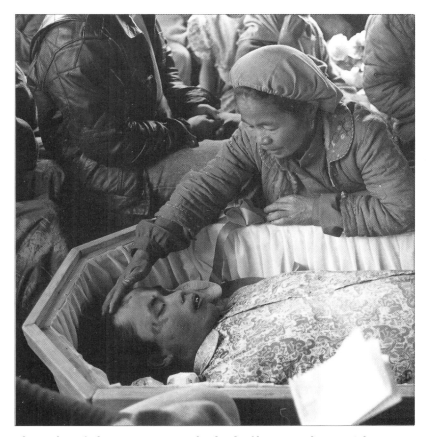

*The mother of Chris Batan mourns the death of her son. A human rights activist and a campaigner for the rights of indigenous peoples in the Philippines, he was killed by members of a government-backed militia in February 1993. Many other defenders of human rights have been killed in the Philippines in recent years.*

An investigation into the killing was opened and, according to reports, in April one of the suspected perpetrators was arrested and the following month charged with murder. However, independent sources said that the five other CAFGU members identified by witnesses as having being involved in the killing were still on the loose and were continuing to harass people in the community.

Three Arhuaco Indian leaders from the Sierra Nevada mountains of Santa Marta, Colombia, were travelling by bus to Bogotá in November 1990 to register an official complaint (*denuncia*) about human rights violations against the indigenous communities of the Santa Marta by the army and police. Luís Napoleón Torres, his brother Angel María Torres and Hugues Chaparro were forced off the bus by three heavily armed men wearing army uniforms and taken away. A fortnight later their three bodies were found dumped at different sites. All showed signs of torture. Such incidents are all too common in Colombia, where those who have tried to stand up for human rights have frequently become victims themselves.

South African David Webster, a 44-year-old anthropologist and human rights activist, was shot dead by gunmen firing from a moving vehicle outside his Johannesburg home in May 1989. Shortly before his death he had published a paper on the development of "death squads" and other forms of covert repression in South Africa.

The police investigation into his death pointed to the hitherto unknown Civil Cooperation Bureau (CCB), a unit falling under the Directorate of Military Intelligence. In another inquiry, a witness named the military intelligence official alleged to have killed David Webster. It also appears that David Webster had discovered evidence of continuing South African military assistance to RENAMO, the Mozambican armed opposition, which could have been the motive for his killing. However, the judicial inquest into David Webster's death concluded in January 1993 without determining the identity of his killers.

Human rights activists in many parts of the world risk death and deprivation of liberty for standing up for what they believe to be right. It is often only because of their courage that human rights crimes become public knowledge — the very reason why they become victims of the violations they are trying to stop.

## Demonstrators

Who can forget the scene in Beijing's Tiananmen Square in June 1989? Millions of people around the world held their breath as army tanks and battalions of soldiers encircled the thousands of brave Chinese men and women who were peacefully demonstrating for democratic reform. The protesters seemed oblivious of the danger — youthful optimism and a determination to defy intimidation kept them unbowed in their makeshift tents.

On 4 June the world watched helplessly as hope turned to despair. The tanks crashed through the streets as they moved towards the square. Soldiers fired indiscriminately into the fleeing crowds. Within hours, the streets of Beijing were littered with bodies and stained with pools of blood. At least 1,000 civilians were killed and many more injured.

The government's response to the slaughter was an extreme example of how officials dispute the circumstances of killings in what can roughly be described as "crowd control" situations. Having first denied that anyone had been killed in Tiananmen Square, it later said that "over 200" civilians had died in Beijing either from stray bullets or as a consequence of soldiers defending themselves from attack by demonstrators.

*The terrible aftermath of peaceful pro-democracy protests organized by Chinese students in June 1989. Bodies lie unattended near Tiananmen Square, Beijing, after tanks and troops swept through the city killing at least 1,000 unarmed civilians. The government claimed no one had been killed in the square, but admitted that "over 200" had been killed in Beijing. There has still been no public inquiry into the massacre. (c) AP*

GETTING AWAY WITH MURDER

*Mourners at the Santa Cruz cemetery, in the East Timorese town of Dili, seen
here peacefully demonstrating their demand for independence for East Timor.
Indonesian troops later fired indiscriminately into the crowds, killing an
estimated 200 people and injuring hundreds of others. (c) Popperfoto/Reuters*

Mass killings of demonstrators and others gathered in crowds
are regularly reported from around the world. In many cases, the
sheer scale of the bloodshed or photographic evidence prove beyond doubt that the intention of security officers was nothing to do
with "crowd control" and everything to do with causing death to
punish and intimidate.

It was a lone cameraman who brought to the world's attention
a massacre at a peaceful gathering of mourners in East Timor. On
12 November 1991, around 3,000 people had assembled at Santa
Cruz cemetery in Dili. They were paying their last respects to a
young man who had been killed by Indonesian troops two weeks
earlier, and were demonstrating for independence for East Timor.
The peaceful atmosphere was suddenly broken by the sound of
semi-automatic rifles being fired. Then came the cries of terror and
the screams of the wounded and dying.

The hundreds of soldiers who had surrounded the cemetery
continued firing into the crowd without interruption for two or
three minutes. Then came short bursts of shooting. A survivor
recalled:

*"Looking down the road I saw body after body, and the
soldiers kept firing at those who were still standing."*

An estimated 200 people were killed and hundreds of others injured. The officials did not bother to count the dead. Instead, the government and military authorities offered a range of excuses for a massacre they could not deny. They said that the soldiers had been "provoked". There had been a "riot". The soldiers had fired when "the mob attacked them brutally". The killings were the result of "a misunderstanding by the soldiers". The soldiers shot because of the "tension". And so on.

These excuses did nothing to dampen the international outcry, so the government set up a commission of inquiry. This proved to be little more than another attempt to cover up the truth.

The Dili killings were clearly extrajudicial executions. All the many witnesses stated categorically that the procession of mourners was peaceful and that the soldiers had opened fire without warning or provocation. Then there was the film.

It is inconceivable that hundreds of soldiers would have decided on their own to go to the cemetery in army trucks and open fire on unarmed civilians. Without access to military files it is impossible to determine who gave the orders, but the failure to investigate the massacre adequately or to bring those responsible to justice indicates that not only was there official complicity at the time, but that the complicity is continuing to this day.

It is often the case that when governments claim that the police or military were being attacked by demonstrators, the evidence points to an entirely different scenario. In May 1990 Indian paramilitary forces killed dozens of unarmed mourners in Srinagar in Jammu and Kashmir state. Government ministers claimed that religious militants mingling in the crowd of mourners had started the shooting by firing at the paramilitary forces and that civilians had been killed in the "cross-fire". Yet numerous witnesses and journalists said the paramilitary forces had fired indiscriminately and without provocation into a crowd of people who were simply trying to pay their last respects to a man who had been shot dead earlier that day by unidentified gunmen.

In the Israeli-Occupied Territories, the killing of Palestinian demonstrators in disputed circumstances continues at an alarmingly persistent rate. Of the approximately 100 Palestinians shot dead in the first five months of 1993 by Israeli forces, including by undercover police and army units, almost 30 were children or youths aged 16 or younger.

Danish Army Major Allan Huglstad, who was visiting Gaza as

a delegate for Amnesty International in May 1993, described a scene he witnessed:

> *"I was standing at the corner of a narrow street, near about 10 youths and boys. These young people were not doing anything other than watching, like me, a patrol of Israeli soldiers who were advancing towards us. When they were more than a hundred metres from us, the soldiers began firing in our direction. I heard no warning and the soldiers appeared to be in no danger. Four or five shots were fired. A bullet hit the dust near me."*

In Madagascar, against a background of increasing protests mounted by an opposition alliance, *Hery Velona*, Active Forces Committee, scores of peaceful pro-democracy demonstrators, possibly more than a hundred in all, were shot dead by security

*At least 37 people, including a 10-year-old boy, were killed and many others injured when soldiers opened fire on a peaceful demonstration in the Zairean capital, Kinshasa, in February 1992. Here, one of the victims is carried away by friends.*

forces between August and October 1991. In August, for instance, at least 30 *Hery Velona* supporters were killed when troops fired into a crowd near the presidential palace in the capital.

In Zaire at least 37 people, including a 10-year-old boy, were killed when soldiers opened fire on a peaceful demonstration in Kinshasa in February 1992. The march, which was organized by Roman Catholics, was calling for the resumption of the recently-suspended National Conference to debate political reform. The government had repeatedly used violence to suppress opposition demands that the President's powers be curtailed: at least 250 people were killed during looting and indiscriminate violence by government troops in September and October 1991, and at least 500 people were killed in late January 1993 in similar circumstances. No official action has been taken against those responsible.

Governments who meet non-violent demonstrations with violence are preventing their citizens from expressing peacefully their grievances. Such responses to protests not only violate fundamental human rights. They can also create an atmosphere in which people who are denied peaceful methods of political participation may opt for violent means. This can only lead to more bloodshed and further abuses of human rights.

## Prisoners

Early one evening in October 1992 several hundred military police stormed the House of Detention in São Paulo, Brazil, to quell a violent disturbance between rival gangs of inmates. Less than 12 hours later 111 prisoners lay dead. About two-thirds of them had been shot in the head and chest. Some 35 others were wounded.

This was how one prisoner described what he saw:

> *"Police came in firing. They opened the door and told us to get out. We said we were unarmed. As one boy got up from the bed to go out a police officer shot at him three times...They fired a shot near the toilet area and killed another one. A police officer called out: 'there are some other ones alive here' and three more police came in with machine guns and fired..."*

The then Secretary of Public Security told the press that in cases of prison disturbances, police are ordered to shoot to kill and there was nothing absurd about police using machine guns against prisoners.

*Some 111 defenceless prisoners were massacred when military police quelled a disturbance in Brazil's House of Detention in São Paulo in October 1992. The bodies were taken from the cells and piled up on the first floor of the prison. (c) Instituto de Criminalistica de São Paulo*

In fact, what happened that day was a massacre of defenceless prisoners. Most of the victims were killed after surrendering. Forensic evidence showed that many appeared to have been killed while lying or sitting down with hands on or behind their heads. Wounded prisoners were shot dead, as were prisoners who were ordered to remove bodies from the cells. Several survivors said they had hidden among the dead bodies and that police had bayoneted the bodies and shot those who cried out.

Eight separate inquires into the massacre were set up. All found that either "excesses" or "military crimes" had been committed, although none attributed individual responsibility for the killings. Nevertheless, the military justice prosecutor brought charges against 120 officers and soldiers for homicide, attempted homicide and grievous bodily harm. In mid-1993 those charged were still awaiting trial and no other action had been taken against them.

Such killings, on a lesser scale, are not uncommon in Brazil where military police, who are answerable only to special military courts, have rarely been successfully prosecuted for killings.

The House of Detention massacre is just one example, albeit an extreme one, of the many ways in which prisoners are killed unlawfully in state custody each year.

States have a wide range of responsibilities, guaranteed in international and most national laws, towards the people they imprison. Yet all too often, prisons are not simply places where convicted law-breakers serve out sentences, but dangerous hell-holes where the lives of inmates are seriously at risk. In all the following examples, the evidence strongly points to unlawful killings of prisoners.

In Venezuela, at least 63 inmates of the Retén de Catia prison in Caracas were killed in November 1992 by members of the Metropolitan Police and the National Guard who raided the severely overcrowded prison to stop a reported escape attempt. Witnesses said the security forces fired at the prisoners indiscriminately. Forensic examinations showed that many victims had been shot in the back. No one has been held accountable for the killings.

One of the most brutal massacres of prisoners took place in Syria in June 1980. Hundreds of prisoners held at Tadmur Prison were summarily killed by Syrian security forces, including members of the *Saray al-Difa'* (Special Defence Units). Most of the victims belonged to the Muslim Brotherhood, membership of which was made a capital offence in Syria the following month.

In Mauritania, over 300 political prisoners were reportedly killed in prisons, military barracks or police stations between November 1990 and March 1991. All were black Mauritanians detained during mass arrests in late 1990. Witnesses said that more than 140 detainees had been executed without trial or tortured to death. A further 200 are believed to have died in custody as a direct result of torture or ill-treatment, including extremely harsh prison conditions, although no specific information is available about what happened to them.

Many unlawful prison deaths around the world are a consequence of inhuman prison conditions often compounded by deliberately cruel, inhuman or degrading treatment.

For example, in Malawi many prisoners are believed to have died in recent years after being beaten, chained naked and denied food during special "hard-core" punishment programs. Towards the end of their sentences, persistent criminal offenders were transferred to Dzeleka or Nsanje prisons where they were forced to run a gauntlet of warders who beat them with clubs, whips and iron bars. Those who survived were chained naked to the floors of their cells and fed one-quarter rations of food. Families of probable "hard-core" punishment victims say the prisoners' clothes were returned to them without explanation — a sign that the prisoner was dead. In 1992 it also appeared that political detainees were subjected to deliberately crowded and insanitary conditions in Chichiri Prison in Blantyre and Maula Prison in Lilongwe. One cell in Chichiri Prison, measuring about five by four metres, was reported to contain 285 prisoners. Former inmates estimated that an average of one prisoner died in this cell every two nights. When a prisoner died, he was immediately replaced by another, suggesting that the authorities were prepared to deliberately perpetuate conditions that resulted in death.

In Côte d'Ivoire, scores of prisoners died in 1992 in the main prison in Abidjan as a result of extremely harsh conditions. Lack of hygiene, inadequate medical attention and insufficient food led to over 100 deaths between February and July alone.

In Sierra Leone, as many as 500 prisoners, most of them Liberians, died in Pademba Road Prison in Freetown as a result of torture or neglect in 1991 and 1992. Nine of 27 Liberian inmates released in September 1992 had been so badly treated in custody that they died in hospital in Liberia within days of their release. Survivors said they had been held in total darkness for the first four months of their detention and denied adequate food and all medical attention. They said many had been tortured to death by the security police and that others had died from malnutrition and disease.

Many hundreds of prisoners die every year worldwide in state custody as a result of torture. State officials in scores of countries use torture methods that are inherently life-threatening, such as electric shocks, drugs, immersion, severe beatings and suspension. Whether death was the aim of the torturers is often difficult to establish, but in several countries the routine and systematic use of the most brutal methods, with consequent high levels of fatalities, indicates that interrogation or punishment cannot be the sole motives. Such is the case in countries such as India and South Africa, where hundreds of detainees have died after brutal treatment in custody in the past decade.In 1992 alone, Amnesty International recorded deaths in state custody allegedly caused by torture or ill-treatment in over 30 countries.

## 'Social undesirables'

Two Brazilian children, 14-year-old Erivan José da Silva and 15-year-old José Fernandes de Almeida, were riding their bicycles in the town of Lagarto, Sergipe, in May 1992. Suddenly, they were grabbed and forced into a car by three men, two of whom were said to be military police officers. It was not an uncommon sight in Brazil's streets. On-lookers had a fairly good idea that the boys would soon be dead.

Their fears were confirmed when the abductors shouted out that this was the last time the children would be seen alive. The next day the boys' bodies were found under a bridge. Their hands were tied behind their backs and they had been shot three times. The only unusual aspect of the case was that two of the military police officers allegedly involved, as well as a civilian, were

*Young and old take to the streets of Rio de Janeiro in November 1991 to protest against the killing of street children in Brazil. Thousands of poverty-stricken children in the country's big cities have been murdered or "disappeared" in recent years by "death squads", often made up of or run by police. (c) Maria Luiza Carvalho*

detained. One officer later escaped but the two others who were held are still awaiting trial.

In recent years thousands of poverty-stricken children in Brazil's big cities have been murdered or made to "disappear" by "death squads", often made up of or run by police officers. Many are killed during "sweeps" aimed at clearing the streets of so-called delinquents. A report published in February 1992 by a Parliamentary Commission of Inquiry of the Federal Chamber of Deputies said that participation of civil and military police in the killing of children and adolescents is "far from exceptional". Despite this, little has been done to stop the almost daily murder of children by government forces.

In Colombia's cities, a successful "social clean-up operation" is official-speak for another night of murder by police or their coliaborators of homosexuals, prostitutes, drug-addicts, vagrants, "street children" and the mentally ill. Such operations are common, particularly in the larger cities of Cali, Bogotá, Medellín and Barranquilla. The assailants often gun down their victims from motorbikes or trucks. Sometimes they round up their catch and force the helpless victims into trucks: the bodies, frequently mutilated, are dumped in rubbish tips or by roadsides.

In July 1992, for instance, a group of teenagers tragically mistimed their departure from a birthday party in the poor neighbourhood of Juan Pablo II in Cuidad Bolívar on the southern outskirts of Bogotá. As they walked down the street, they came face to face with a group of heavily armed men apparently on a "clean-up" operation. The men fired on the group, killing six. Rosabel Jiménez, the grandmother of one of the victims, was shot dead as she tried to catch hold of one of the assassins. A police cap was found under her body.

Statistics for "clean-up operations" in Colombia are hard to obtain as the identity of many victims is not known and deaths go unreported or unregistered. An indication of the scale of such killings was given by local human rights groups, who recorded 298 murders in "clean-up operations" by "death squads" between April and November 1992.

In several countries police routinely use brutal methods and excessive force against people suspected of criminal activities. Often, suspects are identified not by their actions, but by their colour or social class.

In the USA, officers in the Los Angeles Police Department

(LAPD) and the Los Angeles Sheriff's Department regularly use higher levels of force than allowed by law or by their own official guidelines. All too often this force leads to serious injury or death. Victims have been shot, ferociously beaten, attacked by police dogs or "tasered" (stunned with potentially lethal electric shocks administered through a dart gun firing a fine wire). Blacks and latinos have consistently borne the brunt of such brutality. Officers and deputies responsible for causing injuries or death in unlawful circumstances have rarely been disciplined or prosecuted.

The horrific beating of Rodney King in 1992 brought international attention to police brutality in Los Angeles — because a witness happened to capture the assault on video. Many other similar incidents, some resulting in fatalities, have failed to make even the local news.

In July 1992, moments before he was shot dead by a white Los Angeles police officer, John Daniels, a black truck driver, scribbled a note to a garage attendant saying: "If something happens to me, call this number."

According to the attendant, two motorcycle policemen then approached Daniels, who was unarmed, and began arguing with him. Seconds later one of the officers shot him in the neck without warning when he tried to drive slowly away. Daniels, whose father was shot dead by the Los Angeles police in 1985, had claimed that the police had a vendetta against his family. The officer who shot John Daniels was subsequently charged with murder — reportedly the first time in more than 10 years that such a charge had been brought against a LAPD officer acting while on duty. John Daniels' family was awarded $1.2 million in settlement of a civil suit.

In Jamaica there has also been a disturbing number of cases in which criminal suspects or others have been shot by police in circumstances which did not appear to warrant the use of lethal force. In some incidents, suspects have been shot after they had allegedly surrendered or been taken into police custody. In others, people have been killed when the police used guns with reckless disregard for life. Similarly, in Venezuela the casual murder of people living in poor urban neighbourhoods is a routine police practice during so-called anti-crime operations.

Police officers are supposed to protect life. Yet all too often they become the judge, jury and executioner because they are allowed to get away with using unjustifiable levels of brutality and lethal force against those they deem "likely" to be criminals. Police must be held accountable for their actions: those entrusted to uphold the law must not be allowed to believe they are beyond the law.

It is evident that some governments condone the elimination of those they see as "socially undesirable" — where murder is deemed an expedient tool of order. As a short-cut response to social problems like homelessness, poverty and petty crime, they sponsor or condone assassins on the streets, even to commit the wholesale murder of children.

## Targeted communities

The mother of 16-year-old Bieng Ank was telephoned by police in March 1992 and told to come and collect her daughter's body. What she saw was any mother's worst nightmare. The left-hand side of Bieng's head was missing and the rest of the body bore marks of torture. Bieng's grandfather said:

> *"Her body was in pieces. Her hands were torn between the fingers. Cigarettes had been extinguished on her body. Her body was burned all over."*

Bieng's "crime", it appears, was to have been Kurdish. She had been arrested by Turkish police, along with a hundred others, three days before her death in Sirnak Province following disturbances during Kurdish New Year celebrations. Her mother later told a visiting human rights delegation that eight uniformed members of the Turkish Special Team forces and two plainclothes police officers had taken her into custody.

The official version of her death was that she had accidentally been put in a cell with a rifle, and that she had used the rifle to commit suicide. In April 1992 the state prosecutor pronounced suicide as the cause of death.

In every region of the world there are disturbing examples of particular communities being targeted for brutal repression. One place has recently dominated the headlines for the unimaginable levels of carnage suffered by people because of their religion or national origin — former Yugoslavia.

Siniša Glavaševi "disappeared" on 19 November 1991, the day after the Croatian town of Vukovar surrendered to the Yugoslav National Army (JNA) following a three-month siege. The 33-year-old journalist had worked for Radio Vukovar for three years. Despite the intense nationalism of the period, his friends say he was not one of those journalists who "went to war". Rather, the war came to him.

In the last few days of the siege Radio Vukovar staff moved to the hospital for safety. When the town surrendered, hundreds of hospital staff, patients, civilians and unarmed soldiers who had taken refuge in the hospital grounds were detained by the JNA. Around 200 of them are thought to have been extrajudicially executed and buried at Ovara, near Vukovar. Others, reportedly including Siniša Glavaševi, were taken to detention centres in Serbia. Some were released in prisoner exchanges, but over 200 of those taken from the hospital remain unaccounted for. Siniša Glavaševi's wife and nine-year-old son are among those still waiting for news.

Since the fall of Vukovar, atrocities based on national, religious and ethnic hatred have escalated to sickening levels. Armed forces of Serbs, Croats and Muslims appear bent on reaching new depths of inhuman behaviour, as they indulge in an apparently endless cycle of torture, mutilation and slaughter.

*Journalists look down on bodies found in the Croatian town of Vukovar after the town surrendered to the Yugoslav National Army in November 1991 after months of shelling. Thousands of other men, women and children have "disappeared" or been killed by all sides engaged in the increasingly bitter conflicts which continue to tear the former Yugoslavia apart. (c) AP*

The country is littered with the signs of atrocities. Piles of bodies in makeshift graves. Burned out villages. Bloodstained streets. Mutilated corpses lying abandoned in streets.

The survivors speak of experiences no human should ever be put through. Smilja Juši, a Serbian woman married to a Muslim, watched as Serbian irregulars murdered her husband, two eldest sons and three other men outside their home near Zvornik in April 1992. "They made all of us lie face down," she remembers. "They strangled my eldest son with wire. I saw it all."

In March 1992, 15 members of five Serb families were reported to have been massacred by Croatian troops in the village of Sijekovac. A Muslim fighting with Croatian forces who claimed he took part in the massacre described on video how he and other soldiers had also killed over 30 elderly villagers in their homes and raped young women.

In May at least 83 Muslims, including children as young as two years old, were massacred in the village of Zaklopaa, allegedly by local uniformed Serbs who had previously surrounded the village. Jasmina Hodi described to Amnesty International how the Serbs had killed her father:

> "They fired first at his legs, he jumped and they fired at his body. He fell, we saw how he fell and we started to cry. They fired at us and we ran into the house. As soon as we got into the house, they fired through the windows. They fired so much that, when they had stopped, they thought they had killed us."

In June Serbian forces rounded up some 150 people in the town of Mostar. After separating out the women, children and Serbs, they took the remaining men to the morgue at Sutina cemetery. A surviving Muslim witness said he then heard gunfire and later he and another prisoner were forced to carry seven or eight corpses to a rubbish dump near the river Neretva. He later escaped by throwing himself down an embankment. Two months later the police chief of Mostar announced that 150 bodies had been found in mass graves: all had been shot at close range.

Released Muslim prisoners stated that Serb forces had deliberately and arbitrarily killed large numbers of prisoners in camps in Bosnia-Herzegovina in June and July. According to many accounts, during this period prisoners were being killed almost every night in Omarska camp. Many died after being clubbed to death by guards or Serbs allowed into the camp at night. On some nights as many as 30 were allegedly killed. There were also allegations that Serb prisoners had been killed by their captors: for example, Serbian sources said that at least five men held by Bosnian government forces near Konjic died as a result of beatings in June and July 1992.

Such selecting of people for extrajudicial executions on account of their ethnic, national or religious backgrounds is a worldwide phenomenon.

Mass killings of indigenous peoples in the Americas in past centuries have received much attention in recent years. Yet such killings have never stopped. In Guatemala in the 1970s and early 1980s, tens of thousands of non-combatant Indian peasants were killed by the army during counter-insurgency operations. The indigenous communities of Peru, caught in a decade of conflict between government and armed opposition forces, have also continued to suffer abduction and killing on a mass scale. In Mexico, Indians involved in bitter land disputes have been summarily executed by security forces and landowners' gunmen acting with their support.

In Bolivia, deliberate killings of peasants and indigenous leaders by members of the *Unidad Movil de Patrulla Rural* (UMOPAR), Mobile Rural Police, a specialized narcotics branch of the police force, continue to be reported. In May 1992 Emilio Flores Cropa, a young coca leaf grower, was shot dead by UMOPAR members during a raid near Eterazama, Cochabamba Department. Officials said he had been shot during a confrontation with drug-traffickers, but the local Tropical Peasant Workers' Union said that UMOPAR members had fired on peasants as they were running away.

Religious and ethnic communities have been targeted for political killings and "disappearances" elsewhere in the world.

Seenithamby Pillanayagam "disappeared" in September 1990 when he was 24 years old. He was a toddy tapper, collecting the sap of palm trees from which an alcoholic drink is made. On 5 September the Sri Lankan army raided a refugee camp at the Eastern University at Vantharamoolai in Batticaloa District. The camp contained thousands of people, mainly Tamils, who had fled fierce fighting in the region between troops and LTTE forces. During the raid on the camp, the army arrested 159 men, all Tamils, between the ages of 12 and 45. None of them, including Seenithamby Pillanayagam, has ever been seen again.

In Bangladesh, hundreds of non-combatant tribal inhabitants

*Relatives weep over the body of 10-year-old Gerónimo Soyuel Sisay, one of 15 people killed when Guatemalan soldiers opened fire on a crowd of unarmed Tzutujil Indians in December 1990. Tens of thousands of non-combatant Indian peasants have been killed by the army during counter-insurgency operations in Guatemala since the 1980s. (c) Developing World Photos*

of the Chittagong Hill Tracts have been extrajudicially executed since 1989 in the context of a long-running conflict between the government and armed tribal groups seeking regional autonomy. In just one incident, on 10 April 1992, over 100 unarmed tribal people were reportedly murdered in Logang, apparently in a reprisal attack. Paramilitary security forces were said to have set fire to the village and shot dead those attempting to escape.

In Rwanda, 45-year-old Michel Karambizi, his wife and 10-year-old child, were forced out of their house at gunpoint by Rwandese soldiers in October 1990. All three were then shot dead in cold blood. Michel Karambizi was a member of Rwanda's majority Hutu ethnic group who lived in Kaboye, near Kigali, the capital. He and his family were apparently murdered because the government suspected Michel Karambizi's brother of supporting the rebel Rwandese Patriotic Front (RPF), a predominantly Tutsi organization which a few days earlier had launched an attack in northern Rwanda.

In the months following the RPF attack, government forces massacred around 1,000 people in an attempt to crush support for the rebels. Unlike the Karambizi family, most of the victims were Tutsi. Many others "disappeared".

The government said a judicial inquiry was under way into the killing of the Karambizi family, but three years on no findings have been made public. An International Commission of Inquiry into human rights violations in Rwanda since October 1990 published its findings in March 1993. It implicated the government of President Juvénal Habyarimana in the organization of several thousand political killings of government opponents and Tutsi carried out by members of the security forces, armed militias and vigilante gangs loyal to the President's party.

## Victims of reprisals

Forty-three cattle were stolen. Three weeks later 43 men were abducted by a squad of armed men, some hooded, some in military uniform. The abducted men were never seen alive again.

The logic of this reprisal killing was sickeningly simple. The cattle had been hijacked and stolen on the road near Pueblo Bello, a small town in the Urabá region of northwest Colombia. Guerrillas from the People's Liberation Army were blamed. The ranch owner, known locally as "Rambo", accused the people of Pueblo Bello of

*Relatives demonstrate against the "disappearance" of 43 men in Pueblo Bello, Colombia. The victims were kidnapped in early 1990 by armed men, believed to be members of a paramilitary group, in reprisal for the theft of 43 cattle. The ranch-owner, who worked closely with the military, had blamed the armed opposition People's Liberation Army for the theft and accused local people of sympathising with the guerrillas. The bodies of six of the abducted men were later found in a common grave on the ranch. (c) ASFADDES*

sympathizing with the guerrillas. Armed men then swooped on the town, grabbing men from their homes and the local church. One man for each head of cattle. The trucks carrying the abducted men were allowed to pass freely through a military road block.

A month after the abductions, in February 1990, one of the kidnappers gave himself up to the civil authorities. He testified that the 43 men had been taken to the ranch of "Rambo" where they were tortured, killed and buried. The police searched the ranch and found common graves containing 24 bodies. Six were identified as among the 43. The others have not been found.

Soon after the bodies were found, five members of a paramilitary group were arrested and charged with kidnapping and murder. They were released shortly after. In July 1990 the regional prosecutor assigned to the case, Dr Mariá Ester Restrepo Quinceño, and her bodyguard, were shot dead. Four men were arrested, including a police officer who claimed that a soldier from the army's Voltígeros Battalion had supplied the guns. There seems no end to the cycle of killings sparked off by the loss of a rancher's cattle.

In Burundi, soldiers burst into Isidore Ciza's house in Muzinda as they suspected him of sympathizing with insurgents. They found instead a household of terrified children and women, including his first wife, Maria Mawazo, on whom they took a swift and brutal revenge. The soldiers forced the women and children back into the house at gunpoint and then tossed in a grenade.

The blast killed most of the women and children. But that wasn't enough for the soldiers. They re-entered the house and shot each child at point-blank range. Isidore's second wife miraculously survived by hiding under a bed. Among the pile of shattered bodies were 27-year-old Maria Mawazo, 18-year-old Générose Haboni-mana, six-year-old Pélagie Nzeyimana, five-year-old Jean-Claude Nduwimana, four-year-old Anitha Ndayishimiye and baby Guil-laume Ndayisenga.

The slaughter took place in late 1991 during army operations against Hutu insurgents in which as many as 1,000 Hutu civilians were extrajudicially executed. The government claimed the women and children were "victims of cross-fire" and no investigation has been initiated.

Camillo Odongi Loyuk was killed because he left his besieged home town at the wrong time. An elderly civil servant from Juba in southern Sudan, he decided to go to Khartoum to make sure his two daughters were safely in school.

But his visit happened to coincide with a mass "mopping up" operation in Juba in which government soldiers moved from house to house searching for SPLA members. In the previous weeks the SPLA had twice attacked and nearly captured Juba, and the army wanted revenge.

During the operation several hundred young men were report-edly shot dead. Some suburbs were razed to the ground. Among about 100 or so men arrested were several former colleagues of Camillo. They have since "disappeared".

Camillo was arrested in Khartoum on suspicion of having fled Juba to avoid detention. He was taken to an interrogation centre where he was tied spread-eagled to the bars of a window. A rope with a sliding noose was tied around his testicles. When he moved the knot tightened, causing excruciating pain. He was then beaten to death.

A year after the killings a sham investigation had failed to account for any of the missing or dead, including Camillo Loyuk.

In Angola, government troops took violent reprisals in Septem-ber 1992 against the local population in Cabinda. At least six civilians were killed. They included a woman who was shot as she swept her doorstep and João "Incumbio" Macaia, a civil servant, who was burned to death by soldiers — they placed a tyre round his neck, doused it with petrol and set it alight. Later in the year, in early November, government troops and armed civilians deliberately killed hundreds of unarmed civilians in Luanda during house-to-house searches for UNITA members. Witnesses said they had seen bodies with the hands or ankles bound, indicating they had been captured and then killed. Further killings during searches were reported on a lesser scale in other cities.

# 3

## Why the terror continues

As has been shown, governments resort to political killings and "disappearances" when their authority is challenged — at one extreme by powerful opposition political organizations that genuinely threaten to take over, at the other by critics who simply voice their criticism or opposition, or their desire to participate in the affairs of the nation.

So what lies behind the decision to use or allow murder as part of government policy?

Sometimes it appears to be simply a short cut to a desired end. It may seem easier to allow soldiers to shoot to kill suspected members of armed opposition groups than to go through the protracted process of arrest and prosecution.

Similarly, governments under popular pressure to deal harshly with crime can find it politically expedient to order or tolerate "clean-up" operations which are little more than campaigns of assassination against the poor and other "social undesirables". Such "clampdowns on crime" are still claiming lives in countries such as Brazil, China, Indonesia, Pakistan and Venezuela — with very little outcry.

Often, the decision to sanction murder by official forces is a question of habit, inherited from predecessors or simply practised for so long that it has become a way of life for the perpetrators. In Myanmar, for example, the army has been fighting Karen separatists since 1949, routinely using methods which are gross violations of human rights. The abuse of civilians living in Karen areas has become a normal part of daily life for Myanmar's army.

Sometimes the motive appears to be self-preservation (or the maintenance of power and privilege), regardless of the cost. The Chinese authorities, faced with a peaceful pro-democracy movement spreading rapidly across the nation, unleashed whole divisions of the army and tanks to crush unarmed protesters. The months of brutal repression that followed achieved the government's aim — in the short-term at least. A similar motive appeared to drive the Iraqi government to an orgy of murder in response to mass uprisings in the north and south of the country following the Gulf conflict.

Elsewhere, governments which have seized power have turned to the terror of mass murder and "disappearances" to consolidate or maintain their position. A classic example was the military government in Chile, which killed over 2,000 civilians — or made them "disappear" — after ousting the democratically-elected Allende government in 1973. More recently, similar tactics were used by the Haitian military rulers who ousted the elected Aristide government in 1991. At least 1,000 Haitians were extrajudicially executed in the next two years and tens of thousands have attempted to flee the country to escape the carnage.

In some countries, a deliberate and calculated policy to physically eliminate through brutal repression both the armed opposition and entire sectors of the population which the authorities consider disaffected (and so potential supporters of the insurgents) has been the hallmark of government counter-insurgency policies. The policy has had mixed results around the world — sometimes effectively wiping out the opposition for a while, at other times inspiring even greater numbers of people to join the insurgents.

In Sri Lanka mass "disappearances" and political killings appear to have had opposite effects in different parts of the island. In the south, armed opposition was virtually eliminated by 1990 after two years of unbridled terror. In the northeast, however, armed opposition to the government has increased in the past decade, despite the same tactics being used. The authorities have lost control of large areas and the main separatist movement, the LTTE, has grown from a small group of armed men in the late 1970s to a fighting force of many thousands of men and women.

In the Philippines, the newly elected Aquino government introduced a campaign referred to as the "total approach" to counter-insurgency in 1987. The strategy has provided a political and military rationale for human rights violations and created a climate in which they are highly likely to occur. Military authorities have pursued a policy which facilitates the extrajudicial execution of unarmed civilians. One high-ranking officer stated in 1988 that the strategy involved the elimination of the mass base of the New People's Army (NPA) by "isolating" its "above-ground front organizations in the labour, student, urban poor, religious and other

*Bodies of men killed in 1989 by "death squads" near Kandy, southern Sri Lanka, where officially-sanctioned terror had virtually wiped out the armed opposition by 1990. (c) Reuters/Popperfoto*

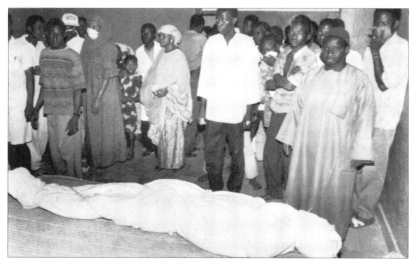

*Relatives and friends mourn the death of a demonstrator in Bamako, Mali. He was one of more than 150 people killed by security forces when pro-democracy protests swept through the country in early 1991. (c) Reuters/Popperfoto*

cause-oriented sectors". In practice, "isolation" has frequently meant "branding" groups of people as equivalent to being guerrillas and giving a green light for "disappearance" or unlawful killing of anyone labelled as a suspected "communist" sympathizer. The campaign, which had failed to achieve its stated objective of destroying the NPA by 1992, has cost hundreds of people their lives solely because of their non-violent beliefs.

Some governments have used political killings and "disappearances" to intimidate the opposition and inhibit any potential opposition. Such is the case in countries like Morocco and the Western Sahara.

In some cases, elected civilian governments appear in practice to rule in conjunction with the military. Such is the situation in Peru. Since early 1983, vast areas of the country have been declared emergency zones under the political-military command of the armed forces. In April 1992, when President Fujimori suspended constitutional rule and closed Congress (with the military's full backing), political analysts concluded that Peru was ruled unofficially by a combined civilian-military government. This system of "dual power" prevents the discovery of the full truth behind gross human rights violations.

Elsewhere, mass political killings have occurred when the state or central government has all but disintegrated. Such has been the case in Somalia and Liberia, where rival armed factions controlling different areas of the country have committed widespread and gross human rights abuses in their attempts to maintain or expand control of territory.

There is a common thread to all these motives — political expediency. Governments which order or condone murder by their forces do so because they decide that their aims can be more easily achieved by such methods than by using peaceful or lawful means, or because it is the only way they can envision to maintain their positions of privilege and power.

Moreover, when governments allow an atmosphere in which human rights can be ignored for political goals, their outcry when opposition groups descend to using the same brutal tactics may just ring hollow. In these circumstances, the chances of peacefully resolving internal conflicts recede even further.

# Impunity

What marks all the disparate scenarios outlined above is the fact that the agents of terror are allowed to get away with their crimes. Perhaps this should not be surprising. They are, after all, at the service of those responsible for "law and order".

In some countries where human rights are most brutally violated, there is little pretence of accountability. In Myanmar, the government has turned the country into a "secret state of terror" in its ruthless crackdown on any opposition. In Iraq, troops have freely massacred civilians, particularly Kurds in the north and Shi'a Muslims in the south. In China, there is no expression of official shame for the violent repression meted out to pro-democracy protesters.

Other governments have barely concealed open invitations to their security forces to kill with impunity when introducing what are ostensibly "emergency" or "temporary" measures. These are said by the government to be needed to combat political violence, but often amount to an official policy to dispense with arrests and to shoot-to-kill with no questions asked.

In India, for example, the Armed Forces (Special Powers) Act, which is in force in several states where there is armed insurgency, gives the security forces wide powers to shoot suspects on sight with impunity so long as the killing nominally occurs in the line of duty. It states: "No prosecution, suit or other legal proceeding shall be instituted...against any person in respect of anything done or purported to be done in the exercise of the powers conferred by this Act."

In Sri Lanka, emergency regulations have at times permitted police to dispose of bodies without autopsies or inquests, making proper investigations impossible to carry out and unlawful killings easy to conceal. The number of "disappearances" and political killings has risen markedly when such a provision has been in force.

In Turkey the dramatic rise in the number of political killings in the past two years has been particularly striking in the 10 southeastern provinces under emergency rule. Under the Emergency Powers Region legislation, complaints brought against members of the security forces for all crimes except murder or attempted murder can only be taken to court with the permission of the local governor's office — the office responsible for security and police affairs. Public prosecutors, who are responsible for investigating killings by security personnel in disputed circumstances, have been extremely reluctant to prosecute members of the security forces for any actions they have committed while on duty.

However, the increasing importance of human rights in international relations means that today there are few governments that openly order their soldiers to commit murder. More common are governments that order covert operations or turn a blind eye to "excesses". When human rights crimes do come to light, those in power go to great lengths to hide the truth and protect the guilty.

The tiny bones of scores of children exhumed by forensic experts at a mass grave in El Mozote, northern El Salvador, in late 1992 were a grim reminder of the atrocities committed during the 12-year civil war that had ended early that year. Survivors of the 1981 El Mozote massacre said that members of the Atlacatl Battalion systematically murdered at least 794 people, many of them children, with machetes, machine guns and knives. Some women were raped before being shot.

For over 10 years Salvadorian officials repeatedly denied there had been a massacre. In 1992 they finally ceded to pressure and allowed the exhumations.

The El Mozote case was among those examined in depth by the UN-appointed Truth Commission, set up under peace accords to look into past human rights abuses by government and opposition forces committed between 1980 and 1982. The Commission said it took direct testimony from several thousand Salvadorians "to contribute to the search for truth as the basis of national reconciliation".

In March 1993 the Truth Commission published its report, which found government forces responsible for massive human rights violations committed during the period of armed conflict. Less than a week later, the President ratified a sweeping amnesty law granting exemption from prosecution to those who committed human rights crimes before 1992. One day later, a colonel and a lieutenant sentenced in 1992 for the 1989 murder of six Jesuit priests, their housekeeper and her daughter, were released under the new law. The colonel was the only senior officer ever to be convicted for human rights violations. Both men had served just 14 months in custody.

In countries all over the world the failure to punish human rights crimes has not contributed to "national reconciliation". On the contrary, it has left the victims and their families with enduring and justified feelings of bitterness, and whole societies in

*The tiny bones of scores of children exhumed by forensic experts at a mass grave in El Mozote, northern El Salvador, in late 1992 were a grim reminder of the atrocities committed during the country's 12-year civil war. For over 10 years the authorities denied there had been a massacre, despite strong evidence that 794 people had been systematically butchered there by the Atlacatl Battalion in 1981. The Truth Commission examined the case and held government forces responsible. In March 1993, less than a week after the commission published its report, the government passed a sweeping amnesty law granting exemption from prosecution to those who had committed human rights violations before 1992. (c) Stephen Ferry*

uncertainty about the future. Moreover, within the security forces, the guilty are still in positions of power and have been given the message that human rights violations can still be carried out with impunity.

Amnesty laws have frequently contributed to both continuing impunity and failures to uncover the truth. Even in Argentina, the best example of former political and military leaders being held to account for past human rights violations, the retreat from full accountability has been rapid. In 1985, five of the military commanders who formed the juntas which ruled between 1976 and 1983 were convicted. They were responsible for the "dirty war" during which over 9,000 people "disappeared". The Argentine government's appointment of a national commission on the "disappeared" and its 1984 report, *Nunca Más* (Never Again), were also pioneering official exposures of the truth. Yet amnesty laws and presidential pardons passed in 1986, 1987, 1989 and 1990 restricted the number of prosecutions and gave immunity to those who acted under orders. These measures also eventually resulted in the release of the five military commanders and other high ranking officers imprisoned for crimes committed during the "dirty war".

In Uruguay, a 1986 amnesty law known as the Expiry Law has meant that no steps have been taken to bring to justice those responsible for mass killings and "disappearances" during the period of military rule between 1973 and 1985. In October 1992 the Inter-American Commission on Human Rights ruled that the law was incompatible with the American Convention on Human Rights.

In Chile, the courts continue to apply an amnesty law which was passed by the former military government to close investigations into cases of human rights violations which occurred before 1978. This is despite the publication in 1991 of the report of the National Commission for Truth and Reconciliation, which documented the massive scale of human rights violations under the previous military government. Similarly, a 1991 law introduced in Honduras granted a broad and unconditional amnesty for certain political crimes, including killings, torture and unlawful arrests committed by police and military personnel.

Various African governments have also granted immunity from prosecution to former government and security officials in order to bring about rapid political settlements. In Benin and Congo, for example, the overall effect of letting particular individuals get away with their crimes has been to avoid a close examination of the systems which allowed them to commit human rights violations, and to avoid reforms. Former President Mathieu Kérékou of Benin, for example, was personally granted immunity from prosecution in 1991, despite the widespread human rights violations that were committed under his government.

Elsewhere, political expediency or weakness has led to the abandonment of attempts to bring to justice past violators. In Niger, for example, an army officer, Captain Maliki Boureima, who was awaiting trial for killing Tuareg detainees in 1990, was released after junior officers took hostage a government minister and the President of the High Council of the Republic in February 1992. The junior officers made several demands, including the unconditional release of Captain Maliki, to which the government agreed in late March 1992. His release appeared to signal an end to attempts by the authorities to hold the army accountable for the extrajudicial executions of hundreds of Tuareg in 1990.

In many countries, there is little sign that human rights crimes will ever be investigated, let alone those responsible brought to justice. A quick survey of some of the political killings and "disappearances" recorded worldwide in recent years shows how many are still uninvestigated and unpunished.

In Afghanistan, after the change in government in April 1992, mass graves of thousands of people allegedly extrajudicially executed under previous governments were discovered. To date, no official investigation has been initiated to discover who was responsible for the mass killings. Similarly, mass graves were uncovered in Zimbabwe in 1992 which appeared to contain the remains of victims of extrajudicial executions by the army in the mid-1980s. Despite this, the authorities refused to open investigations into these killings.

In Mauritania, new information also came to light in 1992 about past political killings. Newspapers published photographs of skeletons identified as those of victims of extrajudicial executions carried out by the National Guard in 1990. Local human rights activists published information about 200 people who had been killed by security forces during expulsions of black Mauritanians the previous year. Despite this, the government took no steps to investigate past extrajudicial executions or to account for hundreds of political prisoners who had "disappeared" in 1990 and 1991. In fact, in May 1993 the National Assembly passed a bill granting immunity from prosecution to members of the national army and security forces for acts committed between 1989 and 1992 — the very period when massive human rights violations were carried out against black Mauritanians.

In Nicaragua, exhumations have continued at sites believed to contain the remains of victims of political killings by government forces during the armed conflict in the 1980s. However, few official steps have been taken to investigate allegations of past abuses, whether by government or opposition (*contra*) forces.

The fate of around 17,000 people listed to have gone "missing" in Lebanon during the civil war of 1975 to 1990 remains unknown and no investigations have been opened. The Yemeni government which took power following the unification in 1990 of the Yemen Arab Republic (YAR) and the People's Democratic Republic of Yemen (PDRY) has done nothing to resolve several hundred cases of past "disappearances". Most of the victims had been detained in the 1970s or in January 1986 in the former PDRY, but 11 had "disappeared" in the former YAR between 1978 and 1985.

Governments also perpetuate impunity by pretending to address past violations by their security forces while actually doing nothing. One common method is to announce investigations into alleged abuses, knowing full well that they will not be allowed to achieve anything. Sometimes the investigation never begins. At other times, it stalls somewhere along the line. Often, the report is simply a whitewash. In almost all cases, the "investigation" becomes a barrier to the truth or a shield for official inactivity.

In Uganda, for example, the present government has announced inquiries into several reported extrajudicial executions by its soldiers. So far, these have only prolonged the army's ability to act with impunity as none of the inquiries has reached any public conclusion.

In Venezuela, judicial investigations into past human rights violations, including political killings by the security forces, have made little progress in the majority of cases. More than 200 cases of death and serious injury caused by the security forces reported in 1989 remained unresolved in the courts.

Similarly, little progress has been reported in recent years in investigations into hundreds of "disappearances" of political activists in Mexico during the 1970s and early 1980s.

Even when investigations are carried out and judicial proceedings started, the institutions responsible for the administration of justice are often weak or inefficient. Frequently, they are susceptible to pressure from other branches of government or the security forces. Prosecutors and judges sometimes behave with outstanding courage, only to flee into exile when their governments are unwilling or unable to protect them from the threats of the accused — usually members of their own security forces.

Such intimidation is frequently reported in Peru. For example, Dr Carlos Escobar, a Public Ministry Special Prosecutor investigating the May 1988 massacre of peasants by the army in Cayara, Ayacucho, received repeated death threats after he submitted a report to the Attorney General in October 1988. His report named an army general as politically responsible for the killing of one of the victims and for crimes against the personal liberty of the others whose bodies were not located.

The process of justice is sometimes subverted by transferring cases to special, usually military, tribunals. For example, in 1989 General Rodolfo Robles, the third highest ranking officer in the

Peruvian army, said that a special military detachment had been responsible for the abduction and massacre of the lecturer and at least nine students from La Cantuta University in July 1992 (see Chapter 1). His signed statement also said that the operation was carried out with the full knowledge and approval of the Commander General of the Army, and named the officers responsible for the planning and execution of the crime.

Despite these revelations, the full truth may never be known and those responsible may never be brought to justice. The case is being investigated by a military tribunal. The tribunal's president, Brigadier General José Picón, reportedly told General Robles: "the General Inspectorate of the Army has reached the conclusion that the army and none of its members had anything to do with this case...so I'm going to stretch it out until everyone forgets about this affair."

That the military tribunal appears to be making little progress should come as no surprise. Despite the massive toll of "disappearances" and political killings in Peru, military tribunals have rarely prosecuted and virtually never convicted military personnel accused of human rights violations. Moreover, once the Supreme Court awards jurisdiction over a human rights case to a military tribunal, the civilian courts are blocked from carrying out independent investigations.

In Colombia and Guatemala, the pattern is similar. Military tribunals generally acquit their fellow officers in cases involving gross human rights abuse. Sometimes the accused even get promoted. Even in the exceptional cases when convictions are secured — usually when the evidence is overwhelming and the case has a high international profile — the punishment rarely fits the crime.

Investigations that fail to be thorough or impartial, or result in derisory punishments, are frequently recorded around the world. Such outcomes do little to deter human rights violators from feeling free to act with impunity.

Official investigations of abuses by Israeli forces in the Occupied Territories since the beginning of the Palestinian uprising in 1987 have generally been inadequate. They rarely result in prosecutions. In the few cases when soldiers or other officials have been convicted, they have received token punishments.

In Nigeria, the January 1991 findings of a judicial commission of inquiry into a police massacre were leaked to the press in late 1992. Eighty people in Umuechem village, in Rivers State in

*Investigators at a mass grave at Cayara, Ayacucho province, Peru, where 30 Indian peasants were massacred by government forces in 1988. Dr Carlos Escobar, a public prosecutor who investigated the Cayara massacre, received numerous death threats after submitting a report which implicated an army general in the killings.*

*These members of a judicial inquiry investigating killings and "disappearances" attributed to army and paramilitary forces were ambushed and shot dead in Magdalena, Medio region, Colombia, in January 1989.*

southeast Nigeria, had been extrajudicially executed in October 1990 by police during protests over land and environmental damage. The commission recommended the prosecution of named police officers responsible for the attack, but its findings were not made public by the government and no police officers were brought to justice.

Another factor reinforcing the confidence of human rights violators was spelled out by the Colombian Procurator General, Dr Carlos Arrieta Padilla:

> *"Perpetrators...calculatedly rely on the mantle of impunity and on the fear of relatives and witnesses preventing them denouncing the "disappearance" themselves, preferring to do it through third parties; all of which means the investigation of this kind of human rights violation is particularly difficult."*

The reluctance of witnesses and relatives of the "disappeared" to report cases for fear of reprisals or because of intimidation is well-founded in Colombia. Those seeking redress have themselves been murdered, "disappeared" or arbitrarily arrested. Even judicial and Public Ministry officials have not been spared such intimidation or brutality. Witnesses, complainants and lawyers in Sri Lanka, Peru and the Philippines have faced a similar fate.

All the factors outlined above contribute to maintaining climates of impunity in which state officials believe they are above the law. Until these conditions are ended, political killings and "disappearances" will continue.

## International apathy

Until Iraq invaded neighbouring Kuwait in August 1990, most of the international community turned a blind eye to the atrocities being committed by the Iraqi government. It ignored the chilling pictures from Halabja, where around 5,000 Kurdish men, women and children were poisoned to death by chemical weapons in 1988. It seemed oblivious of the massacres and the tales of mass "disappearances". It was deaf to the cries of exiles who recounted terrifying stories of the killing and maiming of those suspected of opposing Saddam Hussein's regime.

This blindness was determined by the perception of political and strategic interests many countries had in the oil-rich Gulf. The

*This graveyard in northern Iraq, where hundreds of Kurdish victims of political killings are buried, is a grim reminder of the scale of repression suffered by the Kurdish community in recent years. The international community turned a blind eye to the atrocities being committed by the Iraqi government until Iraq invaded Kuwait in 1990.*

same interests seem to have dictated their actions during 1990 to 1991, even though military intervention to drive Iraq out of Kuwait was said to have been motivated in part at least by human rights concerns. The same governments, having restored the Kuwaiti authorities to power, then failed to prevent them committing widespread violations. Moreover, once the status quo had been restored, the world's attention again shifted away from the continuing human rights crisis in Iraq.

The international community also remained silent while tens of thousands of youths in southern Sri Lanka were "disappearing" or being killed in 1989. Most foreign ministries appeared to prefer quiet diplomacy to public condemnation and attempts to table resolutions on Sri Lanka failed to gain adequate support within the UN.

When the massive and unprecedented scale of the slaughter could no longer be hidden, the European Parliament, Western donor countries and others were stirred to public denunciation. Western donor countries threatened to withdraw aid from Sri Lanka on human rights grounds, and this threat in particular seems to have prompted the government to institute various inquiries and procedures concerned with human rights protection. The government has signalled to the security forces that restraint is required and acknowledged that gross violations have indeed been committed by its forces. This example shows that serious foreign pressure does take place and can have effect. However, the period of greatest abuse remains excluded from the scope of any inquiry so far and serious human rights violations are still being committed, albeit at a lower level.

Elsewhere, governments have given military equipment and other assistance to regimes and their armies which were known to be committing horrific human rights violations while doing little about those violations. The most publicized example of this was the arming of Iraq by European and other governments in the 1980s, at times in defiance of national and international arms embargoes against Iraq. There are, however, many other, less well known cases of human rights concerns being sacrificed on the altar of economic and political gain.

Throughout most of the 1980s, for instance, foreign governments armed, equipped, trained and financed the Chadian security forces when they must have known that their benefactors were systematically butchering defenceless citizens and making thousands "disappear".

Members of Hissein Habré's Presidential Service, a highly trained elite unit repeatedly cited in cases of human rights violations, were trained in Chad by French army officers as well as in Zaire and the USA. The USA supplied Habré's security forces with transport, communications and other equipment, while France, Egypt, Iraq and Zaire contributed financing, equipment, training and intelligence exchange. Other African states cooperated with Chad in intelligence and security operations.

Given this close cooperation, it is impossible to accept that foreign governments did not know what kind of government they were dealing with in Chad — a government which allowed its security forces to slaughter an estimated 40,000 Chadians out of a population of five million.

The international community has declared itself committed to defending human rights. Yet time and again a perverse sense of self-interest has guided governments' responses to human rights crises and has prevented or hindered action in many countries where it is desperately needed. The world has witnessed human rights violations by allies being greeted with silence while those of declared enemies were met with public condemnations, sometimes backed with action. Such hypocrisy can only perpetuate the terror.

This report shows the cumulative failure of nations to make the protection of human rights a genuine priority of government at home and abroad. When governments knowingly shirk their obligation to protect human rights themselves or to hold other states to their international commitments, their seeming indifference becomes complicity. When the international community remains silent, it provides a shield behind which governments believe they can order the state assassins into action with impunity. Conversely, when it brings pressure to bear on governments that persistently flout international standards, all the signs are that at least some respond by attempting to improve the protection of human rights.

## Failure of new governments to confront the past

*"We are not going to be able to investigate the past. We would have to put the entire army in jail."*

Guatemala's former president, Vinicio Cerezo Arévalo, speaking in 1985

Can governments hope to end gross human rights violations if they don't confront the past? That is a key question facing many countries around the world, particularly when new governments take over after years of repression.

Recent history indicates that the answer is no. If serious human rights crimes are not investigated and those responsible not brought to justice, then the climate of impunity which allowed those crimes in the first place is unlikely to change. Moreover, for the victims and their relatives, particularly in cases of "disappearance", the pain and suffering cannot be ended until the crime has been cleared up once and for all.

On the first Friday of every month, a group of women, men and children gather in Tegucigalpa's Las Mercedes Park in Honduras to voice a demand they have been making for over 10 years. They are the mothers, relatives and friends of over 100 people who are believed to have "disappeared" at the hands of the state between 1979 and 1989. Their demand is that the authorities clarify what happened to their loved ones.

No "disappearances" were reported after the government of President Rafael Leonardo Callejas took office in January 1990. Yet his government, like those before it, did nothing to clarify the fate of those who "disappeared" in the 1980s. The President's promises to

*Members of COFADEH, an Honduran organization of relatives of the*
*"disappeared", demonstrate outside the Supreme Court in 1985 as part of*
*their long campaign to find out what happened to their loved ones. In 1993*
*they are still waiting for news, as successive governments have promised and*
*then failed to clarify the fate of over a hundred people who "disappeared" in*
*the early 1980s. (c) Jenny Matthews*

reopen investigations were interpreted as a mockery by relatives
who despair at the failure of the authorities to match their words
with actions.

A leading member of the Committee of the Families of De-
tained-Disappeared in Honduras summed up the feeling of relatives of the "disappeared" in Honduras: "We have been met by a
wall of silence and indifference".

Honduran investigations into the "disappearances" failed to
locate the missing people or bring those responsible to justice. With
internal remedies exhausted, relatives and Honduran human rights
groups turned to the international arena. Numerous cases were
presented to the Inter-American Commission on Human Rights
(IACHR), a body of the Organization of American States. The
IACHR referred four cases to the Inter-American Court of Human
Rights which, despite deaths and intimidation of witnesses, made
unprecedented rulings in 1988 and 1989 finding the Honduran
government responsible for the "disappearances". It found the
government to be in violation of the rights to personal freedom, humane

treatment and the right to life, and ordered it to pay compensation to the families. The government did finally pay some compensation (although not the total amount), but it has yet to comply with the Court's most important recommendation — to investigate and bring to justice those responsible for the practice of "disappearance".

In Latin America and, more recently, in Eastern Europe, the issue of whether to bring to justice state officials responsible for human rights violations under past regimes has at least been widely debated — even if not always acted upon. In Africa, however, there has been little confrontation of the past.

The Chadian government of Hissein Habré ended in 1990. The opposition forces, led by Idriss Déby, swept into power promising to end the years of terror. Nearly three years on and bodies are still being fished out of the River Chari near the capital, N'Djaména. Over 800 people have been extrajudicially executed and dozens have "disappeared". For the latest generation of widows and orphans, President Déby's talk of restoring respect for human rights has been a mockery.

At first the Déby government raised hopes that a new era would begin. A commission of inquiry into past atrocities was set up and its gruesome findings were published. The secret police was dissolved. Political prisoners were freed and democratic institutions were promised or allowed to form.

But the new freedoms were soon under threat. As power struggles within the ruling coalition of armed groups erupted into insurgency, and popular protest against economic austerity and ongoing human rights violations grew in intensity, so reports of killings, "disappearances" and mass arrests began to flood in from Chad. There has been no new era — just a slight pause before the terror resumed. The Déby government, whatever its slogans, has turned to using the very methods of repression it promised to end when fighting the Habré government.

The killers, torturers and abductors are Déby's security forces and one of the reasons they continue to commit these crimes is because no steps were taken to bring to justice those responsible for past human rights violations. Numerous officials allegedly responsible for ordering summary executions under the Habré government have been reappointed to senior posts. President Déby himself was, until 1989, a key supporter of the Habré government and served as army commander in the mid-1980s.

The same immunity from prosecution is still enjoyed in general

*A Chadian soldier stands guard outside the* Camp des martyres, *a military barracks in the capital, N'Djaména, frequently used as a detention centre. Since the Déby government came to power in 1990 promising to end the long-standing pattern of human rights violations, over 800 people have been extrajudicially executed and dozens have "disappeared".*
*(c) Reuters/Popperfoto*

by the present security forces, although the transitional government set up in April 1993 seems to take the problem more seriously. One of its first acts was to set up a commission of inquiry to investigate reports of hundreds of extrajudicial executions in early 1993 in southern Chad. The commission recommended that military officers implicated in atrocities should be brought to justice and that their units should be withdrawn and replaced by units of the Gendarmerie. However, it was unclear whether the government would implement the recommendations and the security forces continue to be under the control of the President.

The consequences of governments failing to confront the past had been seen before in Africa. One place where hopes for a new beginning were perhaps most widely cherished was Rhodesia (now Zimbabwe). There, a white minority government finally conceded democratic rule to the black majority in 1980 after decades of political repression which had culminated in a brutal civil war in the 1970s. During this time, the Rhodesian army, police and other security agencies had been responsible for widespread political killings and "disappearances", as well as other serious human rights violations.

Despite these atrocities, the independence settlement dictated that past violations would not be investigated, that the perpetrators would not be brought to justice, and that the same state officials should be retained in their positions in the security apparatus. The deal, seen as politically imperative to ensure acceptance by the country's economically dominant white community, was to have serious ramifications in the new Zimbabwe.

The legal framework and emergency regulations under which past human rights crimes took place were retained by the Zimbabwean government for 10 years after independence. These broad and arbitrary powers meant the security forces believed they could continue to act with impunity. It also meant that law enforcement officials, such as police officers, failed to gain the basic skills to investigate criminal cases and prosecute them in court. This was particularly serious given the tension and insecurity that existed from the first days of independence.

The new Zimbabwe National Army was formed by integrating members of competing nationalist guerrilla armies and the Rhodesian Army. Rivalry between the former guerrilla armies quickly broke out into open conflict in Matabeleland. In fighting in early 1981, there were several reports of deliberate killings of civilians and prisoners. Many Zimbabweans were disillusioned by the government's use of former Rhodesian soldiers against them during these conflicts. Members of one faction returned to the bush to launch an armed struggle against the new government. Over the next six years there were, once again, gross violations of human rights during the National Army's counter-insurgency campaign against these guerrillas, now officially termed "dissidents".

The government did set up in 1983 a commission to investigate allegations of army killings of civilians in Matabeleland, but its findings were never made public. An official culture of benevolence to perpetrators of human rights violations was ratified in 1988, when under an amnesty the government released 75 members of the security forces who were serving sentences or awaiting trial for human rights violations.

Experience tells us that new governments which offer immunity to former human rights violators, or grant sweeping amnesties in the name of national reconciliation, are often unwittingly damaging prospects for the future. Such actions frequently have the effect of suppressing efforts to determine the truth and perpetuating a climate of impunity.

If "disappearances" and political killings are to be eradicated, today's governments must ensure not only that they are effectively outlawed, but also that past violations are fully investigated and those responsible brought to justice.

# 4

## How to stop the terror

It takes just one key decision to stop political killings and "disappearances" in any particular country. That is the decision by the government to halt them. Once the political will is there, then a series of measures can be implemented which are known to be effective.

In broad terms these are pre-emptive measures to prevent "disappearances" and political killings happening in the first place, coupled with proper investigation and prosecution if they do happen. The latter two measures contribute to prevention by showing public officials in any part of government that their involvement in such crimes is likely to be exposed and punished.

Amnesty International's recommendations for ending the terror of "disappearances" and political killings are summarized in two 14-point programs, which are attached to this report as Appendices I and II. The following section identifies some of the key points in these two programs.

## Prevention

The first, most obvious, task for governments is to make absolutely clear their total opposition to "disappearances" and political killings. They must demonstrate to all police and security forces that such crimes will not be tolerated under any circumstances.

Condemnation must be accompanied by convincing action, including establishing prompt, independent, impartial and effective investigations, and bringing perpetrators to justice (see below). They must disband special units or paramilitary organizations which carry out "disappearances" and extrajudicial executions, and repeal legislation or emergency regulations that prevent victims or their relatives from getting justice and allow the perpetrators immunity from prosecution.

Governments should ensure that both "disappearances" and political killings are criminal offences under national law, with appropriately severe penalties. The law should be broad enough to cover not just the immediate perpetrators, but also those who order, plan, aid or cover-up the crime.

The authorities must make it clear that senior officers who order or tolerate such crimes will be held criminally responsible for human rights crimes committed by those under their command. Government officials should not be allowed to hide behind the excuse that they did not know what was going on or that they could not control the activities of individual officers.

At the same time, members of the security forces must be instructed that they have the right and duty to disobey any order to commit murder or to perpetrate a "disappearance": the old refrain of "I was only following orders" must not be tolerated and must not be accepted as a defence.

Officers who disobey orders expose themselves to the risk of severe punishment. The authorities must establish that a soldier's duty to refuse to commit gross human rights violations takes precedence over the duty to obey orders.

Effective prevention therefore requires proper training for all members of the security forces so that no one can be in any doubt that human rights crimes will not be tolerated. The training should also include education on international human rights standards.

When it comes to the police in the ordinary course of law enforcement, governments should ensure that they are trained to use force only when strictly necessary and only to the minimum extent required in the circumstances as required by international standards. Official guidelines on the use of firearms should specify the circumstances under which they can be used. For example, officers should identify themselves and give clear warnings of their intent to fire, allowing enough time for the warning to be heeded. Detailed reports should follow any use of firearms.

Long experience shows that certain detention procedures often go hand in hand with "disappearances" and political killings and may be designed to evade accountability. Specific safeguards should be implemented for people in custody to make these crimes less likely.

Arrests and detentions should be carried out only by officials who are authorized by law to do so. The officials, who should wear name or number tags, must identify themselves and tell those they arrest why they are being detained at the time of arrest. All this information should be recorded and the records made available to the detainee or his or her lawyer. Details of the place of detention and any transfers should also be made available promptly to relatives, lawyers and courts. All prisoners should be informed immediately of their right to notify family members and others of their whereabouts.

All too often, however, such information is denied to families and friends. If this is the case, those acting on a prisoner's behalf must be able to invoke the power of the courts to locate the prisoner and ensure his or her safety and release if the detention is arbitrary. This internationally recognized principle is based on the widely accepted legal remedy of *habeas corpus*. An individual can ask a court to issue a writ commanding the authorities to produce the prisoner in person before the court. The court can then determine the legality of the detention.

Illegal and arbitrary arrests can be prevented by ensuring that all prisoners are brought before a judicial authority promptly, whether or not a writ of *habeas corpus* or similar order has been issued. Prisoners should also have automatic and prompt access to lawyers, friends and relatives — once a prisoner is seen by concerned people outside it is much less likely that he or she will "disappear" or be killed.

All places of detention should be officially recognized (in other words, not secret) and should be open to regular, independent, unannounced and unrestricted visits of inspection.

When prisoners are released, they should be handed over to someone who can verify the release. Officials involved in "disappearances" sometimes try to cover up the crime by falsely claiming the victim was released.

Ultimately none of these measures will be effective unless the political will exists to make them work. Governments can dramatically improve their human rights records in a very short space of time if they decide to do so.

## Ending impunity

How can governments change the atmosphere in which security forces feel free to butcher, maim and kidnap ordinary people? The first step is to make sure that whenever such crimes are committed, the truth is exposed. The second is to show ruthless determination in bringing the assassins, torturers and kidnappers to justice. Only the fierce light of justice will eradicate the shadow of fear.

As we have seen, many governments and their security forces go to enormous lengths to conceal their human rights crimes. But the truth must be revealed however complicated, expensive or difficult the task proves to be. Not only do the victims and their relatives have the right to know what happened. Exposing the truth is an essential step for ending states of terror.

Investigations must be prompt, thorough and impartial. They must be carried out whenever there is a complaint or some other reliable report of a "disappearance" or political killing.

The main objectives of an investigation should be to establish the facts, to remedy the injustice to the extent possible, and to assemble the evidence that will allow those responsible to be brought to justice.

An official investigation should be run by people independent of those accused of the crime, who must themselves be impartial and protected from intimidation and reprisals. It must have the necessary powers to call witnesses, conduct on-site investigations, and obtain evidence such as government records. It must also have the human and financial resources necessary to do the job.

The investigations should be completed as quickly as possible and the findings made public.

When there is a pattern or long history of serious human rights violations which cannot be tackled in isolation on a case by case basis, then a commission of inquiry with a broad mandate is needed. This must consider the institutional changes required to prevent further "disappearances" and unlawful killings.

Of course, unless investigations are acted on, they have little meaning. At the very minimum, the truth must emerge and those responsible must be brought to justice.

The UN Working Group on Enforced or Involuntary Disappearances summed up what is required as follows:

*"Perhaps the single most important factor contributing to the phenomenon of disappearances may be that of impunity. The Working Group's experience over the past 10 years has confirmed the age-old adage that impunity breeds contempt for the law. Perpetrators of human rights violations, whether civilian or military, will become all the more brazen when they are not held to account before a court of law."*

Impunity can be defined as exemption from punishment. In some instances, it arises from laws or decrees that specifically exempt agents of the state from prosecution. In other cases the suspects are not brought to trial, or they are not convicted despite overwhelming evidence of their guilt. Even when they are convicted, they are sometimes sentenced to derisory punishments, or their sentences are not enforced.

If the problem lies with the law, the law must be changed. If it lies with the weakness of the judicial system, the judiciary must be strengthened and its independence assured.

An effective judiciary must, above all, be independent. Only then can it counteract the abuse of power by government.

The judicial process must be prompt, impartial, effective and fair. Trials should be held in civilian courts, which must be properly resourced.

Because "disappearances" and political killings are such serious crimes, time limitations on prosecution — which often apply to other crimes — should be removed. In other words, there should be no provision which prevents prosecution for extrajudicial executions or "disappearances" after a certain length of time.

The officials behind the crimes — those who planned them, gave the orders or helped to organize them — must be brought to justice as well as the people who carried them out.

Not only must the individuals responsible for "disappearances" and political killings be brought to justice. The state itself must be held responsible if it ordered or acquiesced in the crimes.

What does this mean? It should mean that an international court that examines the case can find the state responsible for a violation under international human rights law and can then order the state to compensate the victims or their families.

This was exactly what happened (albeit a rare example) in the case of Velásquez Rodrígues, a Honduran student who "disappeared" in 1981. The Inter-American Court of Human Rights ruled in 1988 that the Honduran government was responsible for the involuntary disappearance of Velásquez Rodrígues and had thus violated several articles of the American Convention on Human Rights. The Court ordered the government to pay compensation to the victim's next of kin.

In every single country where there is an established pattern of "disappearances" or political killings, impunity is the norm. A determined and consistent government policy of bringing the perpetrators to justice would have an immediate and devastating effect on the minds of past and potential violators. That is why ending impunity is so crucial.

Government officials that proclaim their respect for human rights while allowing impunity to continue must be exposed for the hypocrites they are. Words are not enough. Action is needed.

## International laws, standards and institutions

*"No state shall practice, permit or tolerate enforced disappearances."*

UN Declaration on the Protection of All Persons from Enforced Disappearance, Article 2

*"Governments shall prohibit by law all extra-legal, arbitrary and summary executions..."*

UN Principles on the Effective Prevention and Investigation of Extra-Legal, Arbitrary and Summary Executions, Article 1

Every single extrajudicial execution and "disappearance" cited in this report violated international standards on human rights which all governments have promised to respect.

Such standards mostly began to be set in the wake of the Second World War. Universal revulsion at the horrors perpetrated during that war inspired the formation of the UN in 1945. It was hoped that through this organization governments could resolve their differences peacefully and work together to ensure that human rights atrocities were never again repeated.

The Universal Declaration of Human Rights, adopted in 1948 by the UN, proclaimed that "everyone has the right to life, liberty and security of person" and that no one shall be subjected to torture, arbitrary arrest or detention. These rights apply everywhere, not just in those countries whose governments choose to grant them. This means that all governments are obliged to protect the rights of people under their jurisdiction, and that anyone whose human rights are violated has a claim against the government which violates them. Furthermore, the fact that the world's governments collectively adopted the Universal Declaration means that violations are of concern to all governments, not just those in countries where violations occur.

Since 1948, international human rights standards have been strengthened by the adoption of more than 50 other instruments by the UN. In 1966 it adopted the International Covenant on Civil and Political Rights, which even more explicitly prohibits the arbitrary deprivation of life — a characteristic of the killings described in this report.

In the late 1970s and early 1980s, the UN began tackling the issues of "disappearances" and political killings by governments in greater detail, in response to the enormous scale of these human rights crimes in countries such as Argentina, Cambodia (then Kampuchea), Chile and Uganda.

The discussions eventually led to the adoption of two key instruments: The Declaration on the Protection of all Persons from Enforced Disappearance; and The Principles on the Effective Prevention and Investigation of Extra-Legal, Arbitrary and Summary Executions (see Appendices III and IV). They came into force in 1992 and 1989 respectively.

Both clearly prohibit "disappearances" and extrajudicial executions under international law and specify detailed measures for their prevention and investigation.

To complement UN functions and standards, governments in different regions have created organizations which cover, among other matters, human rights issues. Three of these regional intergovernmental organizations have adopted human rights treaties which are legally binding on the states in those regions which have become parties to them. They are the African Charter on Human and Peoples' Rights, adopted in 1981; the American Convention on Human Rights, adopted in 1969; and the European Convention for the Protection of Human Rights and Fundamental Freedoms, signed in 1950.

All three treaties recognize the right to life and, in particular, the right not to be arbitrarily deprived of life. They also provide for the right to liberty and security of the person, and clearly prohibit "disappearances" and extrajudicial executions. In addition, each provides for the establishment of institutions to supervise its implementation.

Even if international and regional human rights standards did not exist, "disappearances" and political killings would still be unlawful. All national laws proscribe murder as well as kidnapping and abduction.

Those who violate national law are supposed to be accountable before the law. If governments or their officials order, carry out, acquiesce in or cover up "disappearances" or extrajudicial executions, they are violating the very laws which they are supposed to uphold. Similarly, those who violate international law should be accountable before the international community. If governments collectively fail to take action to stop serious human rights violations, they are also violating the very laws which they are supposed to uphold.

Of course, the greatest problem in trying to eradicate "disappearances" and political killings is how to turn accountability into reality.

The UN Secretary-General, Boutros Boutros Ghali, reflected the dilemma facing his organization as human rights crises escalated in 1992:

> "...the UN has not been able to act effectively to bring to an end massive human rights violations. Faced with barbaric conduct which fills the news media today, the UN cannot stand idle or indifferent. The long-term credibility of our organization as a whole will depend upon the success of our response to this challenge."

In fact, from its inception the UN recognized the need for action. For example, the preamble to the Universal Declaration refers to "teaching and education to promote respect for these rights" and "progressive measures, national and international, to secure their universal and effective recognition and observance".

The first substantial resolutions on "disappearances" and extrajudicial executions adopted some 30 years later referred to specific actions which should be taken. One dealing with "disappearances" called on governments to "devote appropriate resources" to searching for the "disappeared", "to undertake speedy and impartial investigations", and to ensure that law enforcement and security agencies are "fully accountable". Another, on extrajudicial executions, called on all governments "to take effective measures to prevent such acts".

The UN has taken measures to secure implementation of human rights standards. These include calling on authorities to conduct impartial investigations into complaints and reports of "disappearances" and extrajudicial executions, to bring the alleged perpetrators to trial and to establish specific safeguards for the prevention of these abuses. Amnesty International believes that these measures are the basic minimum requirements needed to combat these practices and should be undertaken by every government.

The UN has also called for the human rights instruments and their provisions to be incorporated into national legislation, publicized and incorporated in training programs for relevant officials. It has established institutions and procedures to monitor compliance with the standards, make recommendations and take action. It has, moreover, made funds available to governments through UN public information offices and technical assistance programs.

Other action has been taken to combat human rights crimes. The UN has adopted resolutions expressing concern about violations in particular countries and requesting the government in question to take remedial action. It has set up subsidiary procedures — the Working Group on Enforced or Involuntary Disappearances and the Special Rapporteur on Summary and Arbitrary Executions — to deal with particular human rights violations and has entrusted special investigation and monitoring assignments to individual experts (also often called Special Rapporteurs) on particular countries.

More recently it has incorporated specific measures to address human rights in the context of peace-keeping operations, such as those in Cambodia, El Salvador and former Yugoslavia. The concept of on-site monitoring of human rights is also beginning to be developed, as, for example, in Haiti, although this concept is still in the early stages.

None of these UN operations has been free from controversy, however. In former Yugoslavia, the UN has been attacked by various groups both for doing too much and too little. In Somalia, following widespread calls for increased UN intervention, UN forces have been accused of taking sides in an internal conflict and of direct responsibility for human rights abuses.

The UN has also been widely criticized for its inconsistency and selectivity when responding to human rights crises. Four years after the terrible events in Beijing in 1989 and in the face of continuing widespread violations by the Chinese government, the UN has still to take any serious action on China. The Iraqi government was allowed for years to murder thousands of its citizens without censure from the UN — which then suddenly sprang into action after the Iraqi invasion of Kuwait. Other governments responsible for gross human rights violations have also been able to get away without so much as a word of condemnation.

The truth is, however, that the UN's actions are determined by its member states. When member states are guided by narrow political and economic interests, these will be reflected in the decisions taken by the UN. The best human rights standards are meaningless if governments ignore them; the best human rights machinery is powerless if governments refuse to cooperate with it.

Some of these problems were addressed by the World Conference on Human Rights held in Vienna in June 1993. The objectives of the Conference included a review of the UN's mechanisms and procedures in the field of human rights and the formulation of concrete recommendations to improve their effectiveness.

At the Conference, Amnesty International challenged governments to support its call for the establishment of a UN Special Commissioner for Human Rights, with a wide-ranging mandate and the authority to take urgent and decisive action in human rights emergencies. But governments attending the Conference excluded Amnesty International and other non-governmental organizations from the drafting process, where the final document of the Conference was completed in closed sessions by the official government delegations. The resulting Vienna Declaration and Programme of Action failed to give a strong and unified endorsement to the proposal for a High Commissioner for Human Rights or to come up with an agreed framework for the structure and mandate of such a post. Instead, the Conference recommended only that the 1993 session of the General Assembly should begin consideration of the establishment of a High Commissioner as a matter of priority.

Amnesty International and others also called for significant further resources for the UN human rights program, including for the UN Working Group on Enforced or Involuntary Disappearances and the UN Special Rapporteur on summary or arbitrary executions. Amnesty International pointed out that the Working Group on Enforced or Involuntary Disappearances had reported in 1992 a backlog of around 8,000 cases owing to lack of funds. Its report concluded that "...the members of the staff have reached a point where they can no longer cope with the workload," and that "unless additional personnel is assigned to the Working Group, an ever-increasing proportion of the cases received by the Group will not be analyzed, processed and transmitted". Similar complaints were reported by the Special Rapporteur on summary or arbitrary executions. However, the World Conference failed to set any specific targets for an increase in resources and agreed only that additional resources must be found from within the existing over-stretched budget of the UN.

The Conference failed to make any significant contribution to building a world free of human rights violations. Amnesty International's Secretary General summarized the two weeks of discussions as "a summit of missed opportunities". He said: "There has been no reprieve for the victims, as governments fine-tuned their official declarations and reaffirmed the 50-year-old core values of universality, indivisibility and interdependence of human rights." There was no specific reference at all in the Vienna Programme of Action to stronger measures to combat extrajudicial executions and the reference to "disappearances" most disappointingly adds nothing new and makes no new commitments to ways of eradicating these practices.

As in the past, the development of activities on human rights by the UN and regional organizations will depend on the role played by non-governmental organizations such as voluntary organizations, human rights groups, professional associations and other non-official organizations. They have eloquently made known their concerns and called for action. They have supplied the UN with details of thousands of cases of horrendous human rights violations and produced proposals for action which were later adopted by the UN.

The proliferation of international human rights standards and other measures developed by the UN is a step forward, not least because it aids those engaged in campaigns to stop serious human rights violations.

However, the strength of these measures is entirely dependent on the degree to which the governments of the world abide by them. They are not a substitute for government action — the basic responsibility for protecting human rights still lies with individual governments. The continuing nightmare of political killings and "disappearances" can only be ended if governments, both individually and collectively, have the political will to act. Our job is to make sure they do just that.

# 5

## Campaigning for action

Victims of human rights violations are often presented as nameless, faceless statistics. Massacres are rounded up to the nearest hundred or thousand. The individual pain and devastation is lost in the deadening effect of abstract reporting from a distance.

This report aims to show some of the lives behind the lies. It hopes to convey the suffering felt by ordinary people as well as whole communities when governments use terror to achieve their goals. The purpose of the report and the worldwide campaign being mounted by Amnesty International is simple — to stimulate action. Action to stop "disappearances" and political killings.

The people who are behind the crimes are state officials. They take the decisions. They must be forced to change their ways. Our job is to pile on the pressure until they conform to decent and humane standards of behaviour.

What are we asking governments to do?

- We demand that they outlaw "disappearances" and extrajudicial executions.

- We demand that they make it clear that such crimes will not be tolerated at any level, under any circumstances.

- We insist that governments account for victims and promptly conduct full and impartial investigations into all "disappearances" and extrajudicial executions.

- We call for the perpetrators and those who ordered the crimes to be brought to justice.

- We call for compensation to be offered to victims, their orphans, their widowed partners and their families.

We are also asking armed political groups to uphold their obligation to respect basic human rights standards. We call on them to observe international humanitarian standards, specifically to:

- Stop torture and deliberate and arbitrary killings, including killings of civilians and prisoners.

- Release immediately and unconditionally those they hold as hostages and to desist from further hostage-taking.

- Ensure that all those belonging to their organization know that hostage-taking and deliberate and arbitrary killings will not be tolerated, and that those who commit them will be held to account.

Governments have further duties: collectively, through the international community, and individually where they have opportunities to do so, they must take seriously their responsibilities to prevent "disappearances" and political killings wherever they occur in the world. Individual nations must use and support the machinery of the UN and other intergovernmental organizations to stop the bloodshed. They must create international means for bringing perpetrators to justice where national avenues have been closed.

Moreover, no government should ever forcibly return anyone to a country where he or she risks becoming a victim of "disappearance" or extrajudicial execution.

In addition, governments should recognize their responsibilities when exporting arms, training, knowledge and equipment that can be used to commit "disappearances" and political killings. Their legislation on arms and other related exports should prohibit such exports from taking place unless it can be reasonably demonstrated that they will not facilitate human rights violations. Such exports should be publicly disclosed in advance, reports should be issued on the human rights situation in the receiving country, and parliamentary bodies should exercise proper control over the implementation of such laws.

Sadly, however, history has shown that we cannot rely solely on the actions of governments or international institutions to stop abuses.

When ordinary criminals offend, governments deal with them through the process of law. When governments commit crimes or fail to stop human rights violations, who is to discipline them? Amnesty International was set up over 30 years ago to speak out when governments refuse to abide by basic human rights standards. This report shows the terrifying scale of political killings and "disappearances" which is still going on — perhaps the greatest threat to human rights in today's world.

With so many governments trampling on the fundamental rights of their citizens and ignoring abuses abroad, it is up to ordinary people to act. Concerted public pressure can make a difference, even to the most apparently intransigent regimes.

As the Director of the Human Rights Division of the UN Observer Mission in El Salvador said in 1991:

> "...over the past decade non-governmental human rights organizations have played a vital role in protecting and promoting the human rights of the most vulnerable sectors of society, in difficult and sometimes tragic circumstances.... Human rights organizations have been among the few organizations to investigate human rights violations and to protect their victims."

In El Salvador, as in many other countries around the world, the savagery of government repression would never have come to public knowledge without the brave actions of individuals and groups on the ground. They are the wives, husbands, parents and grandparents of the "disappeared" who visit police stations, army barracks and government offices trying to find out what has happened to their missing relatives. They are the community activists, journalists and human rights workers who badger the authorities for information. They are the lawyers who demand their clients' rights. All know the risks they run and some have paid the ultimate price. Without them, the information in this report could never have been compiled and countless human rights violations would remain in the dark.

UN Secretary-General Boutros Boutros Ghali paid tribute to these people last year:

> "In our efforts to build a culture of human rights, we must not forget the importance of human rights workers and non-governmental organizations, nor the courage shown by many who risk their lives and security for the rights of others."

So how can we build a culture of human rights? It means raising and deepening consciousness among officials and the general public about human rights and governments that violate them. It means developing and supporting international and regional institutions which are designed to tackle these violations at source. It means an uncompromising effort to force individual governments to take human rights seriously in their foreign and economic policies. It means insisting that all governments show the political will necessary for decisive action against "disappearances" and political killings at home and abroad.

To achieve this, all those engaged in defending human rights must develop closer links. Often the most horrific violations are allowed to continue because cosy clubs of governments see it could damage their relations with other countries if they took action. We must unite our forces with similar determination — they may have the heavy artillery, but we have the numbers.

This campaign aims to equip that massive human force with one of our few weapons — the facts. It also provides a framework for people, wherever they are, to take up the issues and direct their demands for change at those in power who make the decisions.

Human rights violations are neither natural nor inevitable. We can move forward to a world where governments can no longer get away with murder, where political killings and "disappearances" are exceptional aberrations, quickly stamped out by popular outrage and pressure from the international community. We can create a "new world order" in which basic human rights are a reality for everyone, not a privilege for the few. These goals will not be achieved by wishful thinking. We must take action. Join our campaign today!

# AMNESTY INTERNATIONAL 14-POINT PROGRAM FOR THE PREVENTION OF "DISAPPEARANCES"

The "disappeared" are people who have been taken into custody by agents of the state, yet whose whereabouts and fate are concealed, and whose custody is denied. "Disappearances" cause agony for the victims and their relatives. The victims are cut off from the world and placed outside the protection of the law; often they are tortured; many are never seen again. Their relatives are kept in ignorance, unable to find out whether the victims are alive or dead.

The United Nations has condemned "disappearances" as a grave violation of human rights and has said that their systematic practice is of the nature of a crime against humanity. Yet thousands of people "disappear" each year across the globe, and countless others remain "disappeared". Urgent action is needed to stop "disappearances", to clarify the fate of the "disappeared" and to bring those responsible to justice.

Amnesty International calls on all governments to implement the following 14-Point Program for the Prevention of "Disappearances". It invites concerned individuals and organizations to join in promoting the program. Amnesty International believes that the implementation of these measures is a positive indication of a government's commitment to stop "disappearances" and to work for their eradication worldwide.

## 1. Official condemnation

The highest authorities of every country should demonstrate their total opposition to "disappearances". They should make clear to all members of the police, military and other security forces that "disappearances" will not be tolerated under any circumstances.

## 2. Chain-of-command control

Those in charge of the security forces should maintain strict chain-of-command control to ensure that officers under their command do not commit "disappearances". Officials with chain-of-command responsibility who order or tolerate "disappearances" by those under their command should be held criminally responsible for these acts.

## 3. Information on detention and release

Accurate information about the arrest of any person and about his or her place of detention, including transfers and releases, should be made available promptly to relatives, lawyers, and the courts. Prisoners should be released in a way that allows reliable verification of their release and ensures their safety.

## 4. Mechanism for locating and protecting prisoners

Governments should at all times ensure that effective judicial remedies are available which enable relatives and lawyers to find out immediately where a prisoner is held and under what authority, to ensure his or her safety, and to obtain the release of anyone arbitrarily detained.

## 5. No secret detention

Governments should ensure that prisoners are held only in publicly recognized places of detention. Up-to-date registers of all prisoners should be maintained in every place of detention and centrally. The information in these registers should be made available to relatives, lawyers, judges, official bodies trying to trace people who have been detained, and others with a legitimate interest. No one should be secretly detained.

## 6. Authorization of arrest and detention

Arrest and detention should be carried out only by officials who are authorized by law to do so. Officials carrying out an arrest should identify themselves to the person arrested and, on demand, to others witnessing the event. Governments should establish rules setting forth which officials are authorized to order an arrest or detention. Any deviation from established procedures which contributes to a "disappearance" should be punished by appropriate sanctions.

## 7. Access to prisoners

All prisoners should be brought before a judicial authority without delay after being taken into custody. Relatives, lawyers and doctors should have prompt and regular access to them. There should be regular, independent, unannounced and unrestricted visits of inspection to all places of detention.

## 8. Prohibition in law

Governments should ensure that the commission of a "disappearance" is a criminal offence, punishable by sanctions commensurate with the gravity of the practice. The prohibition of "disappearances" and the essential safeguards for their prevention must not be suspended under any circumstances, including states of war or other public emergency.

## 9. Individual responsibility

The prohibition of "disappearances" should be reflected in the training of all officials involved in the arrest and custody of prisoners and in the instructions issued to them. They should be instructed that they have the right and duty to refuse to obey any order to participate in a "disappearance". An order from a superior officer or a public authority must never be invoked as a justification for taking part in a "disappearance".

## 10. Investigation

Governments should ensure that all complaints and reports of "disappearances" are investigated promptly, impartially and effectively by a body which is independent of those allegedly responsible and has the necessary powers and resources to carry out the investigation. The methods and findings of the investigation should be made public. Officials suspected of responsibility for "disappearances" should be suspended from active duty during the investigation. Relatives of the victim should have access to information relevant to the investigation and should be entitled to present evidence. Complainants, witnesses, lawyers and others involved in the investigation should be protected from intimidation and reprisals. The investigation should not be curtailed until the fate of the victim is officially clarified.

## 11. Prosecution

Governments should ensure that those responsible for "disappearances" are brought to justice. This principle should apply wherever such people happen to be, wherever the crime was committed, whatever the nationality of the perpetrators or victims and no matter how much time has elapsed since the commission of the crime. Trials should be in the civilian courts. The perpetrators should not benefit from any legal measures exempting them from criminal prosecution or conviction.

## 12. Compensation and rehabilitation

Victims of "disappearance" and their dependants should be entitled to obtain fair and adequate redress from the state, including financial compensation. Victims who reappear should be provided with appropriate medical care or rehabilitation.

## 13. Ratification of human rights treaties and implementation of international standards

All governments should ratify international treaties containing safeguards and remedies against "disappearances", including the International Covenant on Civil and Political Rights and its first Optional Protocol which provides for individual complaints. Governments should ensure full implementation of the relevant provisions of these and other international instruments, including the UN Declaration on the Protection of All Persons from Enforced Disappearance, and comply with the recommendations of intergovernmental organizations concerning these abuses.

## 14. International responsibility

Governments should use all available channels to intercede with the governments of countries where "disappearances" have been reported. They should ensure that transfers of equipment, know-how and training for military, security or police use do not facilitate "disappearances". No one should be forcibly returned to a country where he or she risks being made to "disappear".

*This 14-Point Program was adopted by Amnesty International in December 1992 as part of the organization's worldwide campaign for the eradication of "disappearances".*

### AMNESTY INTERNATIONAL 14-POINT PROGRAM FOR THE PREVENTION OF EXTRAJUDICIAL EXECUTIONS

Extrajudicial executions are fundamental violations of human rights and an affront to the conscience of humanity. These unlawful and deliberate killings, carried out by order of a government or with its complicity or acquiescence, have been condemned by the United Nations. Yet extrajudicial executions continue, daily and across the globe.

Many of the victims have been taken into custody or made to "disappear" before being killed. Some are killed in their homes, or in the course of military operations. Some are assassinated by uniformed members of the security forces, or by "death squads" operating with official connivance. Others are killed in peaceful demonstrations.

The accountability of governments for extrajudicial executions is not diminished by the commission of similar abhorrent acts by armed opposition groups. Urgent action is needed to stop extrajudicial executions and bring those responsible to justice.

Amnesty International calls on all governments to implement the following 14-Point Program for the Prevention of Extrajudicial Executions. It invites concerned individuals and organizations to join in promoting the program. Amnesty International believes that the implementation of these measures is a positive indication of a government's commitment to stop extrajudicial executions and to work for their eradication worldwide.

### 1. Official condemnation

The highest authorities of every country should demonstrate their total opposition to extrajudicial executions. They should make clear to all members of the police, military or other security forces that extrajudicial executions will not be tolerated under any circumstances.

### 2. Chain-of-command control

Those in charge of the security forces should maintain strict chain-of-command control to ensure that officers under their command do not commit extrajudicial executions. Officials with chain-of-command responsibility who order or tolerate extrajudicial executions by those under their command should be held criminally responsible for these acts.

### 3. Restraints on use of force

Governments should ensure that law enforcement officials use force only when strictly required and only to the minimum extent necessary under the circumstances. Lethal force should not be used except when strictly unavoidable in order to protect life.

### 4. Action against "death squads"

"Death squads", private armies, criminal gangs and paramilitary forces operating outside the chain of command but with official support or acquiescence should be prohibited and disbanded. Members of such groups who have perpetrated extrajudicial executions should be brought to justice.

## 5. Protection against death threats

Governments should ensure that anyone in danger of extrajudicial execution, including those who receive death threats, is effectively protected.

## 6. No secret detention

Governments should ensure that prisoners are held only in publicly recognized places of detention and that accurate information about the arrest and detention of any prisoner is made available promptly to relatives, lawyers and the courts. No one should be secretly detained.

## 7. Access to prisoners

All prisoners should be brought before a judicial authority without delay after being taken into custody. Relatives, lawyers and doctors should have prompt and regular access to them. There should be regular, independent, unannounced and unrestricted visits of inspection to all places of detention.

## 8. Prohibition in law

Governments should ensure that the commission of an extrajudicial execution is a criminal offence, punishable by sanctions commensurate with the gravity of the practice. The prohibition of extrajudicial executions and the essential safeguards for their prevention must not be suspended under any circumstances, including states of war or other public emergency.

## 9. Individual responsibility

The prohibition of extrajudicial executions should be reflected in the training of all officials involved in the arrest and custody of prisoners and all officials authorized to use lethal force, and in the instructions issued to them. These officials should be instructed that they have the right and duty to refuse to obey any order to participate in an extrajudicial execution. An order from a superior officer or a public authority must never be invoked as a justification for taking part in an extrajudicial execution.

## 10. Investigation

Governments should ensure that all complaints and reports of extrajudicial executions are investigated promptly, impartially and effectively by a body which is independent of those allegedly responsible and has the necessary powers and resources to carry out the investigation. The methods and findings of the investigation should be made public. The body of the alleged victim should not be disposed of until an adequate autopsy has been conducted by a suitably qualified doctor who is able to function impartially. Officials suspected of responsibility for extrajudicial executions should be suspended from active duty during the investigation. Relatives of the victim should have access to information relevant to the investigation, should be entitled to appoint their own doctor to carry out or be present at an autopsy, and should be entitled to present evidence. Complainants, witnesses, lawyers, judges and others involved in the investigation should be protected from intimidation and reprisals.

## 11. Prosecution

Governments should ensure that those responsible for extrajudicial executions are brought to justice. This principle should apply wherever such people happen to be, wherever the crime was committed, whatever the nationality of the perpetrators or victims and no matter how much time has elapsed since the commission of the crime. Trials should be in the civilian courts. The perpetrators should not be allowed to benefit from any legal measures exempting them from criminal prosecution or conviction.

## 12. Compensation

Dependants of victims of extrajudicial execution should be entitled to obtain fair and adequate redress from the state, including financial compensation.

## 13. Ratification of human rights treaties and implementation of international standards

All governments should ratify international treaties containing safeguards and remedies against extrajudicial executions, including the International Covenant on Civil and Political Rights and its first Optional Protocol which provides for individual complaints. Governments should ensure full implementation of the relevant provisions of these and other international instruments, including the UN Principles on the Effective Prevention and Investigation of Extra-Legal, Arbitrary and Summary Executions, and comply with the recommendations of intergovernmental organizations concerning these abuses.

## 14. International responsibility

Governments should use all available channels to intercede with the governments of countries where extrajudicial executions have been reported. They should ensure that transfers of equipment, know-how and training for military, security or police use do not facilitate extrajudicial executions. No one should be forcibly returned to a country where he or she risks becoming a victim of extrajudicial execution.

*This 14-Point Program was adopted by Amnesty International in December 1992 as part of the organization's worldwide campaign for the eradication of extrajudicial executions.*

## UNITED NATIONS DECLARATION ON THE PROTECTION OF ALL PERSONS FROM ENFORCED DISAPPEARANCE

The United Nations (UN) Commission in Resolution E/CN.4/1992/29 of 28 February 1992 transmitted the draft Declaration on the Protection of All Persons from Enforced Disappearance to the UN General Assembly through the United Nations Economic and Social Council (ECOSOC) for adoption. The UN General Assembly adopted the Declaration in Resolution 47/133 of 18 December 1992 "as a body of principles for all States" and urged that "all efforts be made so that this Declaration becomes generally known and respected". The text of the Principles is given below.

### Article 1

1.  Any act of enforced disappearance is an offence to human dignity. It is condemned as a denial of the purposes of the Charter of the United Nations and as a grave and flagrant violation of the human rights and fundamental freedoms proclaimed in the Universal Declaration of Human Rights and reaffirmed and developed in international instruments in this field.
2.  Such act of enforced disappearance places the persons subjected thereto outside the protection of the law and inflicts severe suffering on them and their families. It constitutes a violation of the rules of international law guaranteeing, *inter alia*, the right to recognition as a person before the law, the right to liberty and security of the person and the right not to be subjected to torture and other cruel, inhuman or degrading treatment or punishment. It also violates or constitutes a grave threat to the right to life.

### Article 2

1.  No State shall practise, permit or tolerate enforced disappearances.
2.  States shall act at the national and regional levels and in cooperation with the United Nations to contribute by all means to the prevention and eradication of enforced disappearance.

### Article 3

Each State shall take effective legislative, administrative, judicial or other measures to prevent and terminate acts of enforced disappearance in any territory under its jurisdiction.

### Article 4

1.  All acts of enforced disappearance shall be offences under the criminal law punishable by appropriate penalties which shall take into account their extreme seriousness.
2.  Mitigating circumstances may be established in national legislation for persons who, having participated in enforced disappearances, are instrumental in bringing the victims forward alive or in providing voluntarily information which would contribute to clarifying cases of enforced disappearance.

### Article 5

In addition to such criminal penalties as are applicable, enforced disappearances render their perpetrators and the State or State authorities which organize, acquiesce in or tolerate such disappearances liable at civil law, without prejudice to the international responsibility of the State concerned in accordance with the principles of international law.

## Article 6

1. No order or instruction of any public authority, civilian, military or other, may be invoked to justify an enforced disappearance. Any person receiving such an order or instruction shall have the right and duty not to obey it.
2. Each State shall ensure that orders or instructions directing, authorizing or encouraging any enforced disappearance are prohibited.
3. Training of law enforcement officials shall emphasize the above provisions.

## Article 7

No circumstances whatsoever, whether a threat of war, a state of war, internal political instability or any other public emergency, may be invoked to justify enforced disappearances.

## Article 8

1. No State shall expel, return (*refouler*) or extradite a person to another State where there are substantial grounds to believe that he would be in danger of enforced disappearance.
2. For the purpose of determining whether there are such grounds, the competent authorities shall take into account all relevant considerations including, where applicable, the existence in the State concerned of a consistent pattern of gross, flagrant or mass violations of human rights.

## Article 9

1. The right to a prompt and effective judicial remedy as a means of determining the whereabouts or state of health of persons deprived of their liberty and/or identifying the authority ordering or carrying out the deprivation of liberty is required to prevent enforced disappearances under all circumstances, including those referred to in article 7.
2. In such proceedings, competent national authorities shall have access to all places holding persons deprived of their liberty and to each part thereof, as well as to any place in which there are grounds to believe that such persons may be found.
3. Any other competent authority entitled under the law of the State or by any international legal instruments to which a State is a party may also have access to such places.

## Article 10

1. Any person deprived of liberty shall be held in an officially recognized place of detention and, in conformity with national law, be brought before a judicial authority promptly after detention.
2. Accurate information on the detention of such persons and their place or places of detention, including transfers, shall be made promptly available to their family members, their counsel or to any other persons having a legitimate interest in the information unless a wish to the contrary has been manifested by the persons concerned.
3. An official up-to-date register of all persons deprived of their liberty shall be maintained in every place of detention. Additionally, each State shall take steps to maintain similar centralized registers. The information contained in these registers

shall be made available to the persons mentioned in the paragraph above, to any judicial or other competent and independent national authority and to any other competent authority entitled under the law of the State concerned or any international legal instrument to which a State concerned is a party, seeking to trace the whereabouts of a detained person.

## Article 11

All persons deprived of liberty must be released in a manner permitting reliable verification that they have actually been released and, further, have been released in conditions in which their physical integrity and ability fully to exercise their rights are assured.

## Article 12

1. Each State shall establish rules under its national law indicating those officials authorized to order deprivation of liberty, establishing the conditions under which such orders may be given, and stipulating penalties for officials who, without legal justification, refuse to provide information on any detention.
2. Each State shall likewise ensure strict supervision, including a clear chain of command, of all law enforcement officials responsible for apprehensions, arrests, detentions, custody, transfers and imprisonment, and of other officials authorized by law to use force and firearms.

## Article 13

1. Each State shall ensure that any person having knowledge or a legitimate interest who alleges that a person has been subjected to enforced disappearance has the right to complain to a competent and independent State authority and to have that complaint promptly, thoroughly and impartially investigated by that authority. Whenever there are reasonable grounds to believe that an enforced disappearance has been committed, the State shall promptly refer the matter to that authority for such an investigation, even if there has been no formal complaint. No measure shall be taken to curtail or impede the investigation.
2. Each State shall ensure that the competent authority shall have the necessary powers and resources to conduct the investigation effectively, including powers to compel attendance of witnesses and production of relevant documents and to make immediate on-site visits.
3. Steps shall be taken to ensure that all involved in the investigation, including the complainant, counsel, witnesses and those conducting the investigation, are protected against ill-treatment, intimidation or reprisal.
4. The findings of such an investigation shall be made available upon request to all persons concerned, unless doing so would jeopardize an ongoing criminal investigation.
5. Steps shall be taken to ensure that any ill-treatment, intimidation or reprisal or any other form of interference on the occasion of the lodging of a complaint or the investigation procedure is appropriately punished.
6. An investigation, in accordance with the procedures described above, should be able to be conducted for as long as the fate of the victim of enforced disappearance remains unclarified.

## Article 14

Any person alleged to have perpetrated an act of enforced disappearance in a

APPENDIX III

particular State shall, when the facts disclosed by an official investigation so
warrant, be brought before the competent civil authorities of that State for the
purpose of prosecution and trial unless he has been extradited by another State
wishing to exercise jurisdiction in accordance with the relevant international
agreements in force. All States should take any lawful and appropriate action
available to them to bring all persons presumed responsible for an act of enforced
disappearance, found to be within their jurisdiction or under their control, to justice.

## Article 15

The fact that there are grounds to believe that a person has participated in acts of an
extremely serious nature such as those referred to in article 4, paragraph 1, regardless
of the motives, shall be taken into account when the competent authorities of the
State decide whether or not to grant asylum.

## Article 16

1. Persons alleged to have committed any of the acts referred to in article 4,
paragraph 1, shall be suspended from any official duties during the investigation
referred to in article 13.
2. They shall be tried only by the competent ordinary courts in each State, and not
by any other special tribunal, in particular military courts.
3. No privileges, immunities or special exemptions shall be admitted in such trials,
without prejudice to the provisions contained in the Vienna Convention on Diplomatic Relations.
4. The persons presumed responsible for such acts shall be guaranteed fair treatment
in accordance with the relevant provisions of the Universal Declaration of Human
Rights and other relevant international agreements in force at all stages of the
investigation and eventual prosecution and trial.

## Article 17

1. Acts constituting enforced disappearance shall be considered a continuing
offence as long as the perpetrators continue to conceal the fate and the whereabouts
of persons who have disappeared and these facts remain unclarified.
2. When the remedies provided for in article 2 of the International Covenant on
Civil and Political Rights are no longer effective, the statute of limitations relating
to acts of enforced disappearance shall be suspended until these remedies are
re-established.
3. Statutes of limitations, where they exist, relating to acts of enforced disappearance shall be substantial and commensurate with the extreme seriousness of the
offence.

## Article 18

1. Persons who have, or are alleged to have, committed offences referred to in article
4, paragraph 1, shall not benefit from any special amnesty law or similar measures
that might have the effect of exempting them from any criminal proceedings or
sanction.
2. In the exercise of the right of pardon, the extreme seriousness of acts of enforced
disappearance shall be taken into account.

## Article 19

The victims of acts of enforced disappearance and their family shall obtain redress and shall have the right to adequate compensation, including the means for as complete a rehabilitation as possible. In the event of the death of the victim as a result of an act of enforced disappearance, their dependants shall also be entitled to compensation.

## Article 20

1. States shall prevent and suppress the abduction of children of parents subjected to enforced disappearance and of children born during their mother's enforced disappearance, and shall devote their efforts to the search for, and identification of, such children and to the restitution of the children to their families of origin.
2. Considering the need to protect the best interests of children referred to in the proceding paragraph, there shall be an opportunity, in States which recognize a system of adoption, for a review of the adoption of such children and, in particular, for annulment of any adoption which originated in enforced disappearance. Such asoption should, however, continue to be in force if consent is given, at the time of the review mentioned above, by the child's closest relatives.
3. The abduction of children of parents subjected to enforced disappearance or of children born during their mother's enforced disappearance, and the act of altering or suppressing documents attesting to their true identity, shall constitute an extremely serious offence, which shall be punished as such.
4. For these purposes, States shall, where appropriate, conclude bilateral and multilateral agreements.

## Article 21

The provisions of the present Declaration are without prejudice to the provisions enunciated in the Universal Declaration of Human Rights or in any other international instrument, and shall not be construed as restricting or derogating from any of the provisions contained therein.

## UNITED NATIONS PRINCIPLES ON THE EFFECTIVE PREVENTION AND INVESTIGATION OF EXTRA-LEGAL, ARBITRARY AND SUMMARY EXECUTIONS

At its 15th Plenary Meeting the United Nations Economic and Social Council (ECOSOC) by Resolution 1989/65 of 24 May 1989 recommended that the Principles on the Effective Prevention and Investigation of Extra-Legal, Arbitrary and Summary Executions annexed to the Resolution be taken into account and respected by governments. The United Nations General Assembly subsequently endorsed the Principles by Resolution 44/162 of 15 December 1989 and recommended that the Principles "shall be taken into account and respected by Governments within the framework of their national legislation and practices, and shall be brought to the attention of law enforcement and criminal justice officials, military personnel, lawyers, members of the executive and legislative bodies of the Government and the public in general". The text of the Principles is given below.

### Prevention

1. Governments shall prohibit by law all extra-legal, arbitrary and summary executions and shall ensure that any such executions are recognized as offences under their criminal laws, and are punishable by appropriate penalties which take into account the seriousness of such offences. Exceptional circumstances including a state of war or threat of war, internal political instability or any other public emergency may not be invoked as a justification of such executions. Such executions shall not be carried out under any circumstances including, but not limited to, situations of internal armed conflict, excessive or illegal use of force by a public official or other person acting in an official capacity or a person acting at the instigation, or with the consent or acquiescence of such person, and situations in which deaths occur in custody. This prohibition shall prevail over decrees issued by governmental authority.

2. In order to prevent extra-legal, arbitrary and summary executions, Governments shall ensure strict control, including a clear chain of command over all officials responsible for the apprehension, arrest, detention, custody and imprisonment as well as those officials authorized by law to use force and firearms.

3. Governments shall prohibit orders from superior officers or public authorities authorizing or inciting other persons to carry out any such extra-legal, arbitrary or summary executions. All persons shall have the right and duty to defy such orders. Training of law enforcement officials shall emphasize the above provisions.

4. Effective protection through judicial or other means shall be guaranteed to individuals and groups who are in danger of extra-legal, arbitrary or summary executions, including those who receive death threats.

5. No one shall be involuntarily returned or extradited to a country where there are substantial grounds for believing that he or she may become a victim of extra-legal, arbitrary or summary executions in that country.

6. Governments shall ensure that persons deprived of their liberty are held in officially recognized places of custody, and that accurate information on their custody and whereabouts, including transfers, is made promptly available to their relatives and lawyer or other persons of confidence.

7. Qualified inspectors, including medical personnel, or an equivalent independent authority, shall conduct inspections in places of custody on a regular basis, and be empowered to undertake unannounced inspections on their own initiative, with full guarantees of independence in the exercise of this function. The inspectors shall

have unrestricted access to all persons in such places of custody, as well as to all their records.

8. Governments shall make every effort to prevent extra-legal, arbitrary and summary executions through measures such as diplomatic intercession, improved access of complainants to intergovernmental and judicial bodies, and public denunciation. Intergovernmental mechanisms shall be used to investigate reports of any such executions and to take effective action against such practices. Governments, including those of countries where extra-legal, arbitrary and summary executions are reasonably suspected to occur, shall co-operate fully in international investigations on the subject.

## Investigation

9. There shall be a thorough, prompt and impartial investigation of all suspected cases of extra-legal, arbitrary and summary executions, including cases where complaints by relatives or other reliable reports suggest unnatural death in the above circumstances. Governments shall maintain investigative offices and procedures to undertake such inquiries. The purpose of the investigation shall be to determine the cause, manner and time of death, the person responsible, and any pattern or practice which may have brought about that death. It shall include an adequate autopsy, collection and analysis of all physical and documentary evidence, and statements from witnesses. The investigation shall distinguish between natural death, accidental death, suicide and homicide.

10. The investigative authority shall have the power to obtain all the information necessary to the inquiry. Those persons conducting the investigation shall have at their disposal all the necessary budgetary and technical resources for effective investigation. They shall also have the authority to oblige officials allegedly involved in any such executions to appear and testify. The same shall apply to any witness. To this end, they shall be entitled to issue summons to witnesses, including the officials allegedly involved, and to demand the production of evidence.

11. In cases in which the established investigative procedures are inadequate because of lack of expertise or impartiality, because of the importance of the matter or because of the apparent existence of a pattern of abuse, and in cases where there are complaints from the family of the victim about these inadequacies or other substantial reasons, Governments shall pursue investigations through an independent commission of inquiry or similar procedure. Members of such a commission shall be chosen for their recognized impartiality, competence and independence as individuals. In particular, they shall be independent of any institution, agency or person that may be the subject of the inquiry. The commission shall have the authority to obtain all information necessary to the inquiry and shall conduct the inquiry as provided for under these Principles.

12. The body of the deceased person shall not be disposed of until an adequate autopsy is conducted by a physician, who shall, if possible, be an expert in forensic pathology. Those conducting the autopsy shall have the right of access to all investigative data, to the place where the body was discovered, and to the place where the death is thought to have occurred. If the body has been buried and it later appears that an investigation is required, the body shall be promptly and competently exhumed for an autopsy. If skeletal remains are discovered, they should be carefully exhumed and studied according to systematic anthropological techniques.

13. The body of the deceased shall be available to those conducting the autopsy for a sufficient amount of time to enable a thorough investigation to be carried out. The autopsy shall, at a minimum, attempt to establish the identity of the deceased and

the cause and manner of death. The time and place of death shall also be determined to the extent possible. Detailed colour photographs of the deceased shall be included in the autopsy report in order to document and support the findings of the investigation. The autopsy report must describe any and all injuries to the deceased including any evidence of torture.

14. In order to ensure objective results, those conducting the autopsy must be able to function impartially and independently of any potentially implicated persons or organizations or entities.

15. Complainants, witnesses, those conducting the investigation and their families shall be protected form violence, threats of violence or any other form of intimidation. Those potentially implicated in extra-legal, arbitrary or summary executions shall be removed from any position of control or power, whether direct or indirect, over complainants, witnesses and their families, as well as over those conducting investigations.

16. Families of the deceased and their legal representatives shall be informed of, and have access to, any hearing as well as to all information relevant to the investigation, and shall be entitled to present other evidence. The family of the deceased shall have the right to insist that a medical or other qualified representative be present at the autopsy. When the identity of a deceased person has been determined, a notification of death shall be posted, and the family or relatives of the deceased immediately informed. The body of the deceased shall be returned to them upon completion of the investigation.

17. A written report shall be made within a reasonable period of time on the methods and findings of such investigations. The report shall be made public immediately and shall include the scope of the inquiry, procedures and methods used to evaluate evidence as well as conclusions and recommendations based on findings of fact and on applicable law. The report shall also describe in detail specific events that were found to have occurred, and the evidence upon which such findings were based, and list the names of witnesses who testified, with the exception of those whose identities have been withheld for their own protection. The Government shall, within a reasonable period of time, either reply to the report of the investigation, or indicate the steps to be taken in response to it.

### Legal proceedings

18. Governments shall ensure that persons identified by the investigation as having participated in extra-legal, arbitrary or summary executions in any territory under their jurisdiction are brought to justice. Governments shall either bring such persons to justice or co-operate to extradite any such persons to other countries wishing to exercise jurisdiction. This principle shall apply irrespective of who and where the perpetrators or the victims are, their nationalities or where the offence was committed.

19. Without prejudice to Principle 3 above, an order from a superior officer or a public authority may not be invoked as a justification for extra-legal, arbitrary or summary executions. Superiors, officers or other public officials may be held responsible for acts committed by officials under their hierarchical authority if they had a reasonable opportunity to prevent such acts. In no circumstances, including a state of war, siege or other public emergency, shall blanket immunity from prosecution be granted to any person allegedly involved in extra-legal, arbitrary or summary executions.

20. The families and dependents of victims of extra-legal, arbitrary or summary executions shall be entitled to fair and adequate compensation within a reasonable period of time.